THE

AUTISM
FAQ

Everything You Wanted to Know About Diagnosis & Autistic Life

Joe Biel and Dr. Faith G. Harper,
LPC-S, ACS, ACN

Microcosm Publishing
Portland, Ore

THE AUTISM FAQ
Everything You Wanted to Know About Diagnosis & Autistic Life

© 2022 Joe Biel and Faith G. Harper
© This edition Microcosm Publishing 2022
First edition - 3,000 copies - December 13, 2022
ISBN 9781648411175
This is Microcosm #483
Cover and Design by Joe Biel
Graphs on pages 55-61 by Eliot Daughtry | killerbanshee.com
Edited by Elly Blue

To join the ranks of high-class stores that feature Microcosm titles, talk to your local rep: In the U.S. **COMO** (Atlantic), **FUJII** (Midwest), **BOOK TRAVELERS WEST** (Pacific), **TURNAROUND** (Europe), **UTP/MANDA** (Canada), **NEW SOUTH** (Australia/New Zealand), **GPS** in Asia, Africa, India, South America, and other countries, or **FAIRE** in the gift trade.

For a catalog, write or visit:
Microcosm Publishing
2752 N Williams Ave.
Portland, OR 97227
https://microcosm.pub/AutismFAQ

Did you know that you can buy our books directly from us at sliding scale rates? Support a small, independent publisher and pay less than Amazon's price at **www.Microcosm.Pub**

Library of Congress Cataloging-in-Publication Data

Names: Biel, Joe, author. | Harper, Faith G., author.
Title: The autism FAQ : everything you wanted to know about autistic life/ by Joe Biel & Faith G. Harper.
Description: Portland : Microcosm Publishing, [2022] | Summary: "What's it like to be autistic? As many as one in forty-five people live that reality every day, but our culture remains full of myths, stigma, and dangerous misunderstandings of this type of neurodiversity. This guide to life on the autism spectrum is a must-read for autistic adults, their friends, coworkers, partners, and parents-and for anyone who wants to understand the experiences of many people they meet every day. Joe Biel, who was diagnosed as an adult, writes about what it's like to be autistic, joined by the bestselling Dr. Faith G. Harper who speaks from her experience as a parent, friend, and therapist to autistic people. Their real talk and accessible language discusses a wide range of topics, including the diagnostic criteria for autism and how they play out in practice, what it means for autism to be a disability, and co-occurring conditions like depression and anxiety. They answer many frequently asked questions from neurotypicals, and offer some basic life and social skills that the world doesn't always think to explicitly teach autistic people. Most of all, they affirm the many strengths of the autistic brain and point the way to a world where autism is just another way of being"-- Provided by publisher.
Identifiers: LCCN 2022016363 | ISBN 9781648411175 (trade paperback)
Subjects: LCSH: Autism.
Classification: LCC RC553.A88 B52 2022 | DDC 616.85/882--dc23/eng/20220625
LC record available at https://lccn.loc.gov/2022016363

MICROCOSM · PUBLISHING

MICROCOSM PUBLISHING is Portland's most diversified publishing house and distributor with a focus on the colorful, authentic, and empowering. Our books and zines have put your power in your hands since 1996, equipping readers to make positive changes in their lives and in the world around them. Microcosm emphasizes skill-building, showing hidden histories, and fostering creativity through challenging conventional publishing wisdom with books and bookettes about DIY skills, food, bicycling, gender, self-care, and social justice. What was once a distro and record label was started by Joe Biel in his bedroom and has become among the oldest independent publishing houses in Portland, OR. We are a politically moderate, centrist publisher in a world that has inched to the right for the past 80 years.

Global labor conditions are bad, and our roots in industrial Cleveland in the 70s and 80s made us appreciate the need to treat workers right. Therefore, our books are MADE IN THE USA.

CONTENTS

WHAT'S THE DEAL WITH SOCIAL SKILLS? • 123

HOW DO I NAVIGATE FRIENDSHIP, RELATIONSHIPS, AND DATING? • 153

HOW DO WE CONCLUDE THIS BOOK? • 181

WHAT ELSE SHOULD WE READ? • 187

WHAT ARE YOUR SOURCES? • 188

WHO ARE THE AUTHORS • 191

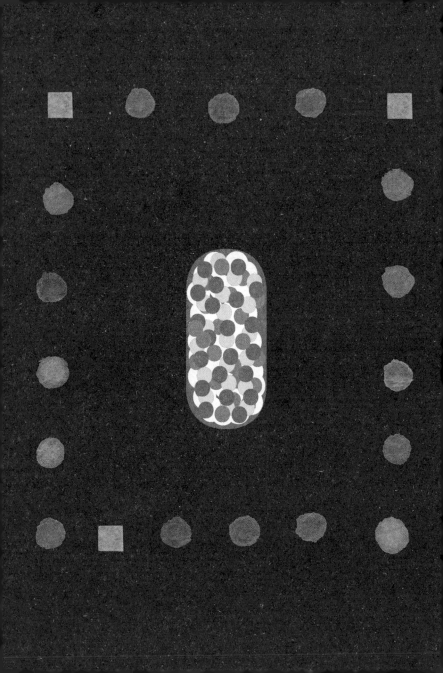

HOW DO YOU EVEN BEGIN?
What is it like to be autistic?

T his morning, as I (Joe) was trying to eat breakfast, a small child kicked the bench that I was sitting on. He kicked it hundreds of times. His parents must have long ago tuned out these repetitive and noisy behaviors. I do not have that luxury. Each kick felt like it was hitting me squarely in the forehead *and* stomach. I had to leave. Negotiating the conversation with the parents wasn't even a consideration. I've tried it before. They would look at me with bewilderment, tell me that he's just a child, and suggest that I ignore it.[1] That sounds like a wonderful privilege.

The previous weekend I had finished building a bookshelf that I had made out of various scrap wood that I'd found by the side of the road. My partner was sick and I needed some help loading it onto my bike trailer to take it to work, so she asked the neighbors. They both came over, almost in disbelief. They stared at me for a full minute, then stared at the homemade bike trailer, then at the bookshelf. Then one of them proclaimed "The series of decisions that you have made here is astonishing." I believe that the statement was meant with respect and acknowledgement, not to be disparaging. They admired the shelf and I explained that I'd made dozens like it, all from materials that I'd found by the roadside. They suggested that their teenage daughter might like one. I believe they also meant this as a compliment but it was not lost on me

---

1 Faith, as a parent of humans, is utterly appalled by this, btw. The kid is just being a kid, but the parents need to work on that home training.

that they were comparing my taste to their teenager's even though I am closer to their age.

My neighbors are likely not autistic. They are likely neurotypicals (NT). That means they live with the privilege of having a brain that works like 98.5% of the population.

Moments like these explain what it's like to be an autistic person. We are undeniably different. We approach problems differently. And you'd be hard-pressed to find two of us who are quite alike. You've likely seen autism referred to as a spectrum. This doesn't mean that some people are "more" or "less" autistic, but that autism affects different people in different ways in different situations at different times with differing impacts. Autism is a pervasive state of being that affects all aspects of our personality, emotions, and experiences. As a result, you cannot separate the person from their autism. It's too wibbly-wobbly timey-wimey for that. Instead of seeking a cure,[2] the solution is honoring and respecting our lived experiences. My partner and my neighbors are pretty good at honoring and respecting my lived experience. Fundamentally, the path to acceptance is building a world that considers and caters to our needs, in the same way that the present world is designed to suit the privileged and powerful.

That leads us to a pretty big task for a not very big book. We are going to talk about what we do know about autism

2 The idea of a cure for autism is a silly idea because it fundamentally misunderstands that our brains are different and that this is a major component of forming our personalities. To "cure" us would be to eliminate us because you cannot separate the other aspects of our personhood from our autism; they are intrinsically interlinked. A more reasonable "cure" would be understanding and acceptance, building a world that suits our needs.

(while freely admitting what we don't know) from a clinical perspective (mostly Faith) and lived experience perspective (definitely Joe). The book is in the format of an FAQ, because we really do get many frequently asked questions about autism. Since this is a singular book and not an encyclopedia, we won't capture everything, which we're sure someone will yell at us about, but we are going to do our best to not miss the big and important stuff. Thank you for being a learn-y nerd with us! Let's get started.

What is it like to care about autistic people?

Hi there, Dr. Faith here. Joe gave me wide margins to fiddle with this book, which I took as an enormous marker of trust. Autism activism is something Joe is deeply passionate about. I stuck to elaborating on brain stuff because that's my wheelhouse. I'm one of those weirdo neurotypicals, after all.[3] This isn't my lived experience. But Joe asked me to speak about my role as a family member of and therapist to individuals who are neurodivergent. And also to be Joe's clinical back up when talking about the science-y stuff. So a lot of that info will have been written by me and all of it will be reviewed by me, like those medical websites where someone with a license reviews the staff writer's content to make sure they didn't put up a picture of scabies and call it a freckle. Or whatever. If either of us are speaking directly using an "I" statement anywhere in the book, we will make sure to tell you who is talking when we do so, as well. But if you aren't sure about anything, feel free

---

3 Some people without autism can still be really interesting and cool. Faith is one example. Our editor, Elly, is another.

to yell at both of us directly and we can decide who deserves it most. As a clinician and an autistic person, we are accustomed to being yelled at.

My Kid #1 is neurodivergent. Their toddlerhood alone was marked by an intense obsession with Frida Kahlo and absolute rage at having any type of clothing touch any part of their skin. This did not make life any easier for a very young single mom who was already at Code Overwhelm. No matter what ideas we have as parents about who our kids are going to be, they come out being exactly who they are instead. And our job is to love that person and help them grow into happy, capable adults. For me, this meant parenting differently and helping aforementioned kiddo learn to navigate a world where most people don't think and process the same way they do.

Fast forward to being a clinician in private practice. My autistic clients are an absolute joy to work with. I *like* working with people who see the world the way they do. It's blissful as a therapist to work with someone who takes my suggestions with logical consideration, decides what makes sense for them to try, and then follows through. The emotionality of neurotypicals and all of our illogical butthurt doesn't come into the picture. I also love how my neurodivergent clients are thoughtful and considerate at an entirely different level, precisely because they *know* they don't have a good read on a situation. The rest of us tend to leap into presumptions about how others are feeling, while my autistic clients are far more inclined to process through it, ask questions, and consider options. I had a client recently spend a session discussing his romantic attraction to his platonic friend. He wanted to make sure his attraction didn't somehow disrespect her or operate as a constraint in their friendship. He wanted strategies to make sure he didn't create discomfort for her because of his feelings. I have *never* had a neurotypical client attend to how their emotional content impacted others in such a considerate manner.

Why did you write this book?

Throughout 2016, after writing *Good Trouble: Building a Successful Life & Business with Autism*, I (Joe) began to be flooded with questions and inquiries about autism. At first I was shocked and overwhelmed because it showed me how much I still had to learn, then I loved it! It was awesome to be able to help dozens and dozens of friends, strangers, friends of friends, and friends of friends' co-workers' children as they suddenly revealed themselves to be autistic. And it was awesome that my big reveal helped them to feel comfortable enough to make their own.

Parents wanted advice about how to interact with their kids. Teens wanted to figure out how to ask people out. Managers wanted to know how to be respectful while motivating and setting expectations for their employees. Parents wanted to know how to help their other children understand their autistic child and to help them grow up with autonomy. There were days where I got little else done because I received so many questions.

But slowly, over time, the questions started to repeat. The answers would repeat as well.[4] Over the next six years, another interesting shift happened: autism awareness began to spread. Slowly, in its wake, autism acceptance followed. Without a changing stigma, I realized that *Good Trouble*, while it contains a lot of advice and key information, couldn't answer everyone's questions.

Dr. Faith Harper and I put our heads together and created *The Autism Relationships Handbook*, since those were by far the most common questions. We have more books coming out as well, but there's a lot of errata that doesn't fit within those confines so, on a whim one day, I decided to compile a wider swath of answers to really get past people's biases and misunderstandings of autism.

The result was a zine that we've expanded to become the book you're reading right now. It's intended for people exploring their own neurodivergence as well as friends, family members, coworkers, and partners of autistic people who want to understand them a little better without making them be responsible for all your education (thanks for doing your own outside learning, btw, appreciated). Also? If you are anything like us, you are tired of misinformation and want to be armed with some facts when someone starts speaking stupid and you need to bring the receipts when you correct them.

---

4 Despite the platform being recently overrun by conservatives repeating misinformation, Joe used to be a prolific poster on Quora.com, so you can find many of these answers in their underedited infancy there, as well as thousands of other answers about all manner of topics!

All of the questions in the following pages are real questions that were posed to me (Joe). Like with any marginalized group, a lot of the neurophobic discrimination against autism comes from autistic people who have been made to look down upon, fear, and hate this aspect of themselves their our whole lives. Overcoming a lifetime of being told that we are lesser isn't done in a day, so I've done my best to infuse humor here to better emphasize that we aren't some dreadfully dreary people who can only do arithmetic. And perhaps part of my joking is to practice for my future text *How to Humor with Autism*. Until then, feel free to get in touch with questions not addressed here. Maybe they'll end up reprinted in the next edition.

And if you are an autistic person, it can be difficult to understand that other people are learning and while their actions may be hurtful or harmful, the baseline for understanding autism is pretty low. There hasn't been a reliable place to get accurate information about autism. So if the other person is amenable to learn, a hurtful conversation with a well-meaning yet ignorant person can be a rare opportunity to fill in the gaps for someone who is willing, interested, and wants to do better. We hope you can use this book to gather your facts and talking points for these conversations.

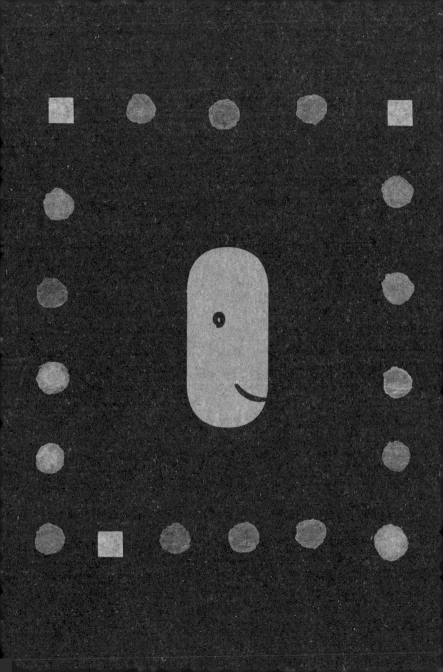

WHAT IS AUTISM?

What is the history of autism?

Here's a brief history of our "discovery" of autism that students get when I'm teaching (Faith here, in case you were wondering).

Autism is not a new diagnosis. It's been in use for about 100 years. The word "autism" comes from the Greek word "autos," meaning "self." The term describes conditions in which a person is removed from social interaction—hence, an isolated self. Eugen Bleuler, a Swiss psychiatrist, was the first person to use the term. He started using it around 1911 to refer to one group of symptoms of schizophrenia. We've known about autism for over 100 years, but originally thought it a form of childhood-onset schizophrenia, which sorta made sense at the time.

In the 1940s, researchers in the U.S. began to use the term "autism" to describe children with emotional or social problems. Leo Kanner, a doctor from Johns Hopkins University, used it to describe the withdrawn behavior of several children he studied. At about the same time, Hans Asperger, a scientist in Germany, identified a similar condition that came to be called Asperger's Syndrome.[5] But even through

---

5 "Asperger's Syndrome" was recently bundled in as Autism type-1 in the DSM-5 because society's understanding of the similarities increased and because of Hans Asperger's work in Nazi eugenics programs (which was based on U.S. ideas about eugenics espoused by Madison Grant). Herr Hans was a public promoment of racial hygiene, which is an in-polite-company term for forced sterilization and even "euthanasia" of children. He was total Scheißdreck. The attempts to shed that history have been awkward and clumsy, but worst of all, these eugenicist ideas delayed autistic diagnosis in the U.S. for decades because of the idea that anyone

the 1960s, treatment professionals thought autism to be a form of schizophrenia: a thought disorder where one sees/hears/smells/feels things that others do not see and believes things that are empirically false. Once there was a realization that autism was a different form of neurodivergence that did not include symptoms of a thought disorder, treatments focused on punishing curative strategies, like electroshock therapy and LSD. It wasn't until the 1980s that treatment professionals started looking at behavioral strategies and adaptations to learning environments to help autistic people live their best lives possible in a neuronormative world.

How do you "get autism?"

OK, still Faith here. Autism refers to a broad range of neurodevelopmental differences that impact someone's ability to communicate, interact, and regulate their nervous system. This may seem slightly vague, but everyone does their humaning differently, including autistic people. And we will also get a little more granular with that definition in just a sec.

The *developmental* part though? Super important. It means "something you are born with." Everything that we are is either something we are born with or something we acquire. Much of what we term "diagnoses" (mental or physical health) can be either, right? You can be born with a heart defect or you can acquire one for a multitude of reasons. Autism is something you can only be born with. You can't fall into a puddle of it. Or bang your head and wake up with it. You can't get a bad batch

with the diagnosis was lesser.

of DMT from a sketch dealer, have a nasty trip, and whoopsie-daisy you are now very very autistic. You either came out that way or you didn't.

Autistic people are born with a brain that works differently. Sometimes those differences are evident immediately, and sometimes they don't appear until someone is 18 to 24 months. But the differences are evident, if only in hindsight, by age three.

So if autism is something we are born with, what causes it? Fuck if we know. There is a heritable component, either genetic or epigenetic. But that doesn't account for all the cases of neurodivergence. Please don't even ask if autism is caused by vaccines. If neurodivergence has always existed in human history and vaccines are a relatively new science, then quite obviously not.[6]

Autism can in no way be traced back to one singular origin. But many of us still struggling with a diagnosis (whether ours or that of someone we love) want answers. If there were a simple answer with a simple solution, we'd have a good inkling by now. However, life is messy and the etiology of autism is just as messy as the vast majority of diagnoses we use to label individuals. Don't forget that fewer than 5% of all human diseases are linked to a singular, faulty gene. Life is almost always way more complex than that. Autism is not a disease within which a non-autistic person resides.

---

6 This theory is propagated by the fact that anyone can publish anything, regardless of its truthfulness. In 1998, Andrew Wakefield published a study of only twelve children in *The Lancet,* claiming that vaccines were causing autism. Others ran with the idea, it was repeatedly disproved, then repeated some more. Let's move on now.

Okay, but what actually is autism?

For the pop culture set, there's *Rain Man* who convinced the world that if I (Joe) *really* were autistic, I would be lying face down on the floor performing experimental calculus equations in my head. I do experimental calculus for fun sometimes but I don't often do so while lying face down on the floor. Carpets usually don't smell that fresh.

Being autistic involves hundreds of encounters where "friends" and strangers alike tell you "You don't seem like you are autistic" or "are you sure that you are autistic?" If you respond by asking a few journalistic questions like "What do you mean?" or "Can you explain?" they often soon realize that they don't know what autism is or how it functions. More important, they cannot fathom what autistic life is like.

Generally autism involves variations on nine things:

- We have about 42% more resting brain activity than most people. Our senses and our brains notice more stuff. Sometimes that's light or heat or visual detail or flavor. One doctor called this "Sensory Issues." Another called it the "Intense World Theory." This is why autistics have filled vital roles in history like inventors, composers, problem solvers, and developers. We are good at noticing stuff and imagining a different approach to it.[7]

---

7 This might be why Joe is so successful as a book publisher, running the fastest growing company in 2022 according to *Publishers Weekly. publishersweekly.com/ pw/by-topic/industry-news/publisher-news/article/89118-fast-growing-independent-publishers-2022.html*

- We get exhausted because of all of this information. This results in needing time alone, stress symptoms, and meltdowns.

- 98.41% of other people are a cryptic, irrational mess who make no sense. Which is how Joe says "not autistic." Doctors call this aspect of autism "difficulty socializing."

- We operate based on a series of complex and elaborate rules that get more complicated every day. Life is like a to-do list and we check a lot of boxes. It feels like other people are messing with us all the time.

- It's hard to understand what other people are thinking or feeling unless they tell us in plain, exact language or we have a lot of history together. For some reason, most people are very uninclined to do either of these things. Other people sometimes feel like we are messing with them. Doctors call this difficulty understanding others a deficit in our "Theory of Mind."

- Stimming is present in almost all autistic people, according to researchers. Some people find ways of doing it subtly, as to not make others uncomfortable, but we're doing it. It's also a pretty regular occurrence during any random week and trying to suppress this behavior has been correlated with an increase in psychological harm. Meaning, it serves an important purpose in nervous system regulation. When I was a child, I "cleaned up" my Legos every day by organizing them into a row. This was comforting to me but psychologists call it "purposeless," because apparently comfort isn't a purpose.[8] Stimming is something all autistic people have in common, though it takes many different forms. I was also comforted by spending hours feeling the texture of a torn-up, dirty blanket. It brought comfort to my small, chaotic world. Naturally, it was destroyed in the washing machine when my neighbors got lice. Now I instinctively say the name of my dog or play with my hair or rub my fingers together. There was a fad around autistic people using fidget spinners for this purpose recently. Most of us open and close our hands repeatedly or make repetitive motions of flapping our appendages. Doctors call this stuff "stimming" as it helps us to relax and be present in our bodies.

- We are fixated on cool stuff. When I was five I liked dolls and action figures. Then I loved legos deeply. For a year I glued together models of dinosaurs and recited every fact about them. Soon I abandoned that for Dungeons & Dragons but that was a little too social for me so I found punk rock and memorized all of the facts about that. Then I became a publisher 27 years ago and fortunately have been able to turn that into a new, exciting adventure every day. I often realize that I've been talking about this stuff for way too long to someone who is politely disinterested and doesn't

---

8 Jokes aside, the reason that autistic comfort is deemed "purposeless," is because psychology is more interested in the comfort of parents and the status quo than autistic people. This is an example of ableism in the framework. It doesn't make sense to them; thus they conclude that it doesn't serve a purpose.

know how to kill the conversation. Doctors call this "Persistent, intense preoccupations."

- Periodically I find myself in a social place full of people where no one will talk to me. I try to spark conversation but people don't want to engage. Sometimes I apply for a job, contract, or speaking gig and have better qualifications than the job requires but they hire someone less qualified anyway. The missing piece is that I cannot see how others see me. I cannot see the outside view of how my amalgamated choices have "bad optics." In short, I look like a sloppy mess who is a bit of a loose cannon or wild card. I cannot see this because I see each of my choices as separate, individual things rather than the composite that they create. On rare occasions I ask someone what happened and they point out a series of very specific and seemingly irrelevant things that I did and said. They explain to me that these things are immature and that other people notice these patterns and make judgments about me as a result. Sometimes these polite, patient people also explain to me how my composite choices actually drive me *away* from my goals. For example, I want to be a successful clinical therapist but instead of getting down to business, I just keep sweeping this one part of the floor and organizing my desk and waiting for people to come to me. It's hard for autistic people to break goals down into actionable steps and see their actions the way neurotypicals (NTs) do. Doctors call this "Executive Function."

Are autistic people sociopaths?

No. We tend to have very dull mirror neurons—or at least the regulatory systems that manage the mirror neurons aren't doing a great job. Meaning we are not great at neuroception, a polyvagal theory term coined by Stephen Porges that refers to the brain's ability to detect the intent of others without conscious thought. So we struggle to read and experience other people's feelings, body language, nonverbal communication, and mental states. People who don't experience neuroception are often read as cold, withholding, or in other ways emotionally withdrawn, disconnecting, or even abusive. It's very hard for NTs to understand that we aren't doing this on purpose, so autism is frequently equated with sociopathy.

In practice, it's the opposite. A sociopath is very emotionally perceptive and thus very adept at manipulating and exploiting the emotions and weaknesses of other people, while an autistic person is completely clueless in this department and does not mean to selfishly bumble through causing harm, though the impact can be just as great. Researchers agree with my perception that we have tremendous—even greater than the average population—capacity for empathy, though it can be harder to access.

We are lacking a window into other people's worlds until they tell us what it's like to be them. It often takes some very plain language to make others' experiences and feelings relate to our own. As we age, we learn to intellectually mimic "performing" empathy through recognizing patterns and behaviors, but this is an extremely draining amount of emotional labor for us to perform. It's also important to point out that our struggles with neuroception mean that along with struggling to connect and relate, we are at higher risk to be taken advantage of by others. Those instincts that tell others to move away from dangerous people are tied to neuroception, so we simply don't have the skills.

Is autism a disability?

When I (Joe) was first diagnosed at 32, the doctor strongly urged me to see autism as a way to understand my situation, not as a set of limitations or a statement about my potential.[9] I was old, accomplished, and experienced enough at this time that I was going to continue on my path in life with this new roadmap of understanding. However, many younger autists' parents have a tendency to coddle them, further causing them to see themselves as functionally incapable of living normal lives. When I became involved with my local chapter of the Autistic Self Advocacy Network (ASAN) I fully grasped this concept. Many of the attendees had been told that acquiring advanced degrees would secure them jobs, but they didn't know how to go about socially pursuing employment. They didn't know how to network. Others followed the directions of social services organizations to the letter and still weren't getting the help they promised. It was difficult to understand that there are unspoken rules, that it isn't fair that we are

9 In social services in Oregon, the term "Person with Potential" is applied to developmentally disabled people. It's patronizing because it implies that we are underperforming, but it amuses me to think about all of these people without potential. Neurotypicals can be so inspiring in their use of language and their averageness!

discriminated against, and that we have to locate points of entry to succeed. Organizations do not always function like they claim to, and goals can be rather nebulous. Having a vision for your life that you cannot achieve is emotionally crushing. It feels like it's your own fault, and it harms your self-image as you watch your peers accomplish the things they set out to do. Strategically, you have to find your own points of entry because the world is not designed to help us. Autistic people have greater trouble understanding these nuances.

Faith here. The dictionary definition of disability is "a physical or mental condition that limits a person's movements, senses, or activities. The prefix "dis-" means lack of or none. So dis-ability means *lack of ability*. You will see the phrase *developmental disability* used regarding autism quite frequently. And while we agree with the term "developmental," the term "disability" can go fuck all the way off with itself. As the National Institute of Health in the UK states, autism is not a disease or an illness. It is the term we use for a large group of people in society whose brains work differently. Autism more accurately falls under the category of *neurodivergence*. Neurodiversity refers to the normal variation in the human population of brain function and behavioral traits associated with that function.

Disability is a concept based on ideas developed by abled people in the "medical model of disability"—that is to say, people who don't have these problems are judging us as inferior. In the "social model of disability," we'd consider instead how the world would be arranged differently for autistic people to thrive, as the current world is designed for neurotypical people to thrive. As one of Joe's mentees explained it, autism is like using a computer with Linux, while being neurotypical is like using a computer with OSX. Neither one is "normal" or "better." Each one has different advantages and they don't always communicate very well with each other.

Society isn't built to be supportive for neurodivergent individuals. It's kinda like . . . the average cis woman in the US is 5'4 and the average cis man is 5'9. The world is built for some variation within that, right? But not a lot. Once you're an adult under about 4'10 or over about 6'5 you start to have issues. You don't fit in well. Things aren't made for you. You can't reach anything or you smash your head on everything. Good fucking luck on public transport. Clothes that fit you off the rack? Not likely. Don't get us started on shoe shopping.

There are plenty of people who are a standard deviation or two away from average, but the world is built for average-or-reasonably-close-to-it. Does this seem fucked up to you? It does to us. If you agree that short and tall people should be able to move comfortably in society? You're already with us. Autism is very much the same thing. It doesn't require "treatment" and it is not something to be "cured" (insert Arnold in Kindergarten Cop yelling "it's not a tumor!"). However, society and all of us within it need to make space for all of our normal variations of being human.

Back to Joe. There's a lot written about how autism is a disability. I bought into this for nearly a decade because, yes, autism makes every aspect of life much more difficult on a daily basis. But within the past year I came to understand that autism is only a disability because of the ways that we are treated every day in response to our autism. The disability is the lack of understanding, being forced to be subjected to toxic and torturous environments that are exhausting with no end in sight.

For most of my life, before I was diagnosed, the disability I experienced was how others perceived my outward expression. For the most part I had a peculiar gait. When I relaxed my hands, I resembled a Tyrannosaurus Rex. I spoke in a monotone. I didn't understand humor or figures of speech. I struggled to socialize with other kids by the time I was ten. I didn't understand when someone was subtly trying to redirect me or refuse my request. I was relentlessly made fun of for things that made no sense at the time and make even less sense now.

The disability is that when we think we have a sympathetic ear, we are told to deal with it; to suck it up; to *recognize our own privilege.* Ironic, considering that privilege refers to *a lack of obstacles.* And I was directly referring to the obstacles I was experiencing. Consequently, I internalized all of that as self-hatred for most of my life. I thought that I was lesser; a fuck up; and that I didn't deserve love or success. I took on the low expectations that others put on me as well as feeling the constant pressure and increased stress that we face every day until we pass out or explode into a meltdown.

I came to realize that being autistic is constantly doing relational labor for everyone around us. It's connecting the dots and reframing each situation for others. Since people are unwilling to take the time to understand us, it becomes our burden to understand them. It becomes a constant process of understanding what sets us off and how to recognize it before it's too late. This isn't fair, and in many ways *that* is the best way of explaining autism as a disability: the way that others treat us and the way that it somehow becomes our job to make up for that. However, demanding that the world become fair overnight isn't a hill that I'm willing to die on. I'm much more interested in creating a life that I want to lead and not subjecting myself and others to poor treatment.

In this way, we can set our own boundaries and show others what are and are not acceptable ways to treat us.[10] We can allow or remove people from our lives based on how they treat us and understand these issues. Slowly, this earns respect and at least pushes people away who are not willing or ready to respect our personhood.

What words are okay to use to describe autistic people?

In one cartoon by the Autistic Avenger, the left panel depicts a person carrying a ball with the caption "person with autism." The right panel depicts a whole person with the ball inside their head and the caption "autistic person."

This concept is difficult and confusing for many well-meaning people who spent years ingraining themselves with the "person first" language popularized by the second wave of the

10 Faith wrote *Unfuck Your Boundaries* if this is a thing you need in your life. And it does explicate why boundaries are so difficult for neurodiverse peeps. And, oh yeah, Joe published it.

disability rights movement. Person-first language means not defining someone by their traits, behaviors, or descriptor. You might say "person driving a car" instead of "driver" or "person who frequently makes exasperated and excited comments" instead of "shouter." In some cases, this is desirable, when people don't want to be defined by a temporary or externally imposed condition like homelessness, a broken leg, or having the divorce rates of a person who commutes in a car. However, autism is different. The autistic community has repeatedly declared that their personhood is *not* separate or removable from their autism. So we are "autists," or "autistic people" instead of "people with autism."

When "Asperger's syndrome" was removed from the DSM-5 in 2013, many autistic people balked. It was how they thought of themselves; an important part of their identity. For this reason, some people hold onto this label, and that's their choice. But for most, it will slowly disappear. We are just "autistic people" now.

Like any marginalized population, so many things have been taken from us and so many things have been defined on our behalf, framing our terms instead of letting us speak for ourselves. Like any other marginalized group, there is a continual debate about reclaiming language around how autistic people are described, including slurs, to be reframed in a positive light.

Words matter—especially words that have been used to harm people like us since before we were born. We know that emotional trauma causes as much inflammation in the body as physical trauma. Diminishing the power of another human by using othering language is considered a weapon, known in academia as "a slurring speech-act." When the term becomes embraced by the marginalized group and becomes used to self-reference without being derogatory, the term has then become defanged. It is now a reclaimed speech-act, which is empowerment without any bodily violence or broken glass.

The word "queer" was historically a derogatory one. But has been reclaimed to the extent that you can now study queer theory in college. But there are also people who still don't like or use the world because of how the word was weaponized against them in their past.

A person can have negative labels placed on them and disagree with this stigma, remaining proud of who they are. And reclaiming language to be used in a flattering way is a part of that. It may make you uncomfortable, and if you're neurotypical, it should. It's not about you. It's about us. Like most aspects of autistic life, it's about facing the trauma and mistakes of the past. Don't if you don't want to, but consider that for many people the act of language reclamation is as empowering to them as you not using the word at all.

We also don't use terms in this book like "spectrum" (unless we're talking about the clinical term) or "high-functioning" and "low-functioning," for reasons we'll explain in more depth later on. Why? The short answer is that due to how ableism is internalized, especially among autistic people, "spectrum," is often used as a way of avoiding saying that you are autistic because of the shame and stigma around that word.

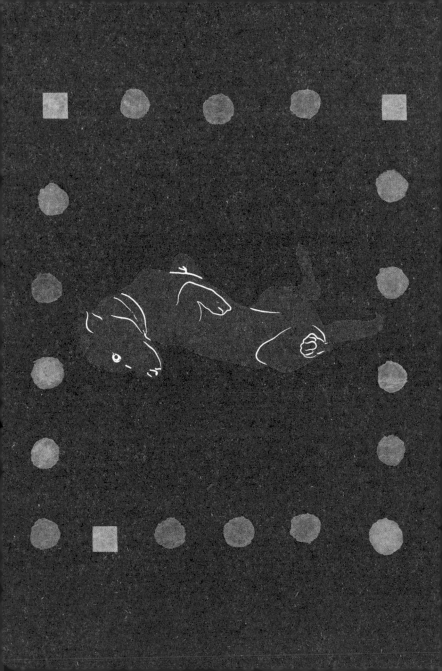

HOW DOES AUTISM DIAGNOSIS WORK?

How does autism get diagnosed?

If you are thinking this feels very "it me" and are wondering what a diagnosis entails, let's talk about what the diagnostic criteria are. Faith not only does assessments and diagnostic impressions, she also teaches this topic, so consider her your Ms. Frizzle for this section, ok?

There are two big categories of diagnostic criteria that clinicians look at when diagnosing autism (or Autism Spectrum Disorder, as it's officially called):

- Deficits in social communication and social interaction

- Restricted, repetitives patterns of behavior, interests, or activities

Let's look at what each of these means.

Deficits in social communication and social interaction have to happen across multiple life domains. Meaning not just in certain situations. Someone who is shy in large groups may have social anxiety . . . and that's not the same thing. Or if they don't talk in school it could be because they are being bullied or their teacher is an asshole or whatever. It has to be a problem in multiple areas of their life. And it can look like a lot of different things, like:

- Struggling with back and forth in conversations

- Struggling with initiating or responding to social interaction

- Struggling with eye contact, facial expressions, or nonverbal communication in general (expressing it or understanding it in others or both)

- Struggling to adjust their behavior to suit different social contexts

- Not being interested in making friends or not being able to make friends

The DSM-5 (that's the fifth edition of the Diagnostic and Statistical Manual of Mental Disorders, the official text from which all mental health diagnoses are made) points out that "social communication and social interaction" is a huge category and these are only examples and not meant to be a complete list.

OK, now what does the DSM mean by **restrictive and repetitive patterns of behavior?** Again, this can be a lot of different things and it's not a full list, but examples include:

- Repetitive bodily movements, or use of objects or speech (like having to spin or flip or line up objects, repeat words or phrases, move hands or feet in certain ways, etc)

- Needing sameness in routines

- Having intense and restrictive interests in subjects or objects

- Having strong reactions to sensory data (either over- or under-stimulated by smells, touch, lights, sounds, movement, etc.)

To be diagnosed with autism, these ways of being in the world needed to be present early in life, even if the individual wasn't diagnosed early in life. It also has to be significant enough to cause problems in school, work, social life, family life, etc. And the issues have to not be better explained by other diagnoses. Autism can co-occur with another diagnosis (and in fact often does), but it is important to make sure that in looking at diagnostic possibilities that it is not (for example) Rett Syndrome, selective mutism, intellectual differences, a developmental delay, or something that can seem similar to ASD. For example, someone who struggles with the social communication part but not the behaviors part should be evaluated for Social (Pragmatic) Communications Disorder when they don't meet criteria for Autism Spectrum Disorder.

What happened to all of those "Autistic-Lite" diagnoses, like Asperger's Syndrome?

Halfway through a phone conversation with a friend, I (Joe) mentioned being autistic and it was like someone scratched the needle on the record. Everything stopped. *WHAT? You're autistic? Since when?* I reminded him of my diagnosis over ten years ago. He said, "That was Asperger's Syndrome, Joe." Like I couldn't keep my diagnoses straight. I told him that it's the same thing and silence filled the call as that detail sunk in.

Since the DSM-5 was published in 2013, the way we think about autism has changed a lot. Many misconceptions have been cleared up—two big ones were the idea that only children could be diagnosed as autistic and the stigma against autism diagnosis that led to a number of more euphemistic diagnoses.

Previously, using DSM-5, patients could be diagnosed with three separate disorders: Autistic Disorder, Asperger's Syndrome, or Pervasive Developmental Disorder—Not Otherwise Specified (PDD-NOS). Additionally, Childhood Disintegrative Disorder (CDD) and Rett's Syndrome were also often used. Researchers found that these separate diagnoses were not consistently applied across different clinics and treatment centers, so they combined them. Anyone diagnosed as autistic, Asperger's or PDD are now considered part of the Autism "spectrum." CDD and Rett's were removed from the spectrum category and Social (Pragmatic) Communication Disorder (SCD) was added as a communication disorder for individuals who struggled with the social part but not the behavioral part.

Under the DSM-5 criteria, individuals with a diagnosis of Autism Spectrum Disorder (ASD) must show symptoms from early childhood, even if those symptoms are not recognized until later. This criteria change encourages earlier diagnosis of ASD but also allows people whose symptoms may not be fully recognized until social demands exceed their capacity to cope to receive the diagnosis. It is an important change from DSM-IV criteria, which was geared toward identifying school-aged children with autism-related disorders, but not as useful in diagnosing younger children.

And despite the common clinical misconception, growing up in a chaotic environment (or any kind of environment where your differences were not noted, or did not present to an extent that it was problematic) doesn't disqualify you from a diagnosis. A good diagnostician can pick apart what is a trauma reaction and what is autism (and we will go more into those differences later, if you're curious). Diagnoses are always based on impact on life domains. It's less important that symptoms exist, and more about how these symptoms affect your ability to navigate society. Maybe you grew up in an environment where no one paid much attention to what was going on with you. Or you were labeled a troublemaker or bad kid, despite the fact that you intended with all your heart to fit in and do well. So if you settle down in your twenties and are trying to maintain a job and a relationship and it's exceedingly difficult because of your neurodivergence, you may still qualify for a diagnosis.

The gold standard for early detection of autism is called the M-CHAT-R. And the American Academy of Pediatrics recommends that pediatricians screen all children at 18 months. Despite this, of the children diagnosed with ASD, only 20% receive their diagnosis before their second birthday.

How do I prepare for my diagnostic appointment?

Faith here. This is a huge question that Faith and Joe both get asked regularly. Getting an actual diagnosis, especially if you are already an adult (at least chronologically), is an exhausting endeavor. A study published after the move to the DSM-5 estimates that a good 25% of autistic children remain undiagnosed. And that's with *better* diagnostic criteria, research, and understanding.

So for those of us who are older, the chances of a diagnosis having been missed is likely much higher. The overall numbers haven't even been estimated effectively, though one study in 2019 demonstrated that 10% of individuals diagnosed with ADHD as a child were actually recognized as being autistic by adulthood. And plenty of researchers have pointed out that many other autistic individuals have had their symptoms misattributed as a different diagnosis.

The system is an imperfect one. It isn't covered extensively in grad school programs and many clinicians don't feel well equipped to diagnose it properly. I have assessed many people over the years who were told by another clinician, "Yeah, I think you might be neurodivergent but that really isn't my area so I'm not comfortable making that judgment."

Whether for yourself or a loved one, getting an accurate diagnosis for *anything* is an exhausting and frustrating experience. If I could help everyone reading this book directly, I would. But since I am only licensed in Texas and have a perpetually full schedule to boot, I'm going to try to help you indirectly with the tips I share regularly.

1. Make a timeline of your behaviors/signifiers of neurodivergence. Anything you remember about your childhood up through the present that may be related. It might be more overt, like you were always stimming by wiggling your toes in your shoes. And it may be more subtle, like a teacher in 3rd grade who

was always accusing you of playing dumb and you remember truly not understanding what she wanted. You have to demonstrate that these symptoms have always existed, and are not the result of some illness or injury in adulthood.

2. Gather any records you do have. Old school records, health records, etc. While they don't have this diagnosis in them, they can help demonstrate patterns and symptoms that were present all along that weren't clocked as neurodivergence. Documentation that shows that you didn't talk until you were three, or always had notes in elementary schools that you struggled to make friends, whatever. If you can get your hands on this information to back up your recounting, it may really help.

3. Fill out an assessment. The one I use as a starting point in my practice is called the AQ-50. It's a self-assessment looking at markers of autism. It's super easy to find online and print. I'd suggest doing that, filling it out, and bringing it with you to your therapy appointment. If you have someone you spend a lot of time with (partner, roommate, family member) you could ask them to fill one out for you, too, based on what they know of you. Even if the clinician you see has you complete different assessments or none at all, anything you bring in becomes part of your file so you now have a diagnostic paper trail going. It also shows you're being serious and thoughtful, not freaking out because there was a viral Tik-Tok announcing that if your third toe

is taller than your second toe, it means you are autistic and have death-butt cancer, or whatever.

4. Ideally, you can find someone who specializes in assessment and diagnosis of neurodivergence. Most websites and clinician advertising platforms (like Psychology Today or Therapist.com) list their specialties. If you aren't sure, it's entirely OK to ask. You're busy and the therapist is busy. If you say you are seeking a diagnosis and ask if assessing and diagnosing autism is in the clinician's wheelhouse, and they say no? Everyone's time just got saved. And if it isn't, but it's a clinician you trust/respect? Ask them who they would suggest. There are plenty of things I'm not good at, but I know which of my colleagues are, and I don't at all mind sharing a recommendation.

5. Consider what you want to do with your diagnosis. Are you just wanting to know/understand yourself better? Use it to direct your mental and physical health care? Are you hoping that will be helpful to your relationships and want to work with a couples or family counselor? Are you hoping to use the diagnosis to get an ADA accommodation (or 504 plan if you're under 18)? Applying for disability benefits? Be clear with the clinician about not just what you are seeking but what you are seeking it for.

6. Charges for an assessment and diagnosis can vary wildly. If you are paying out of pocket, it may be a couple hundred dollars or a few thousand depending

on where you live, the number of sessions the clinician needs, and any other specialized testing that needs to be done. If you have insurance, finding someone who takes your plan can take a while but could save you a ton of money. If you don't have insurance *or* money (welcome to the US!), the strategies we discuss later on for finding skills training services can be of benefit for finding diagnosis and counseling services, as well.

I know, the process seems intensive and likely aggravating. It only seems that way because it absolutely, factually is. Clinicians are having to go back and learn something they already had paid to learn and weren't given. Potential clients are having to fight for adequate care when they should be able to just show up and receive care. Advocacy for improvements in access and care is hugely necessary for all of us, so keep fighting for important changes.

As a clinician, how can I do a better job giving autism diagnoses?

I (Faith) get it. I didn't learn shit about autism in grad school either, beyond "it exists." But this isn't a rare diagnosis and you will absolutely have neurodivergent clients who need care.

First of all, discussing the possibility of an autism diagnosis isn't a shitty or mean thing to say to someone. I mean, as long as you aren't being shitty and mean in the process. A 2019 study of adults who were not diagnosed until they were in their 50s found that getting a diagnosis was a positive experience. It helped them understand themselves and how they interact with the world around them and it shaped their ability to express their needs to their therapist and receive the kind of treatment that was truly helpful for the first time. And I think this is something most of us can relate to. Where something was wrong and we didn't know what and we were scared and confused and kept trying to make things better and instead they just continued to get worse. And then when the "something" part is finally figured out, the relief is palpable and we finally feel like we are headed in the right direction.

So how do you get started in being an effective diagnostican and therapist to neurodivergent clients? You definitely need more training in the area, I know I did. There are more and more trainings being provided online these days, which is incredibly helpful to our schedules and wallets. It's also valuable to consult with a clinician who specializes in this area. Being part of a consulting group in general is really helpful (and I strongly suggest doing so on general principle), but you can also consult with a wise clinical elder. But make sure you pay them (or at least offer to) if you are doing more than asking a quick question that can be answered in under five minutes.

There is also plenty of work you can do on your own to feel more comfortable with recognizing neurodiversity.

1) Get super familiar with the diagnostic criteria. Along with that, get to know the Cultural Formulation Interview in the DSM. It's actually really good, but I'm starting to suspect the only people who are familiar with it are my former students. Understanding cultural norms and how they interplay with mental health issues and their expression is something you should be

doing with all diagnostics. For example, a kiddo who is quiet and not making eye contact with you may not be autistic/anxious/depressed but instead showing respect for you as an elder.

2) Get familiar with neurodiversity screener tools. There are plenty that are easy to use and are a good starting point for discussion, just like we have for depression, anxiety, PTSD and the like. I use the Autism Spectrum Quotient (AQ-50) as a dialogue starting point.[11] It's designed for adults who do not have an intellectual difference. There are plenty of others, including the Ritvo Autism Asperger Diagnostic Scale-Revised (RAADS-R) which has 80 questions, 64 of which are behavioral specific and it's also relatively easy to score. For the itty-bitties there is the M-CHAT-R, as well as plenty of other tools you can use if you work with older children, such as the Ages and Stages Questionnaire (ASQ) and the Parents' Evaluation of Developmental Status (PEDS). If doing these assessments yourself is not your cup of tea, find out who does more intensive assessment and diagnosis in your area so you can refer out.

3) Read. Like, a lot. Books by people with lived experience and books by people who specialize in this work.

4) Spend time with other media. Follow individuals who talk about neurodiversity on social media

---

11 There is also a shorter version, the AQ-10. It's not as robust in terms of reliability and validity, but if you know getting 50 questions answered isn't going to happen, it'll work.

(#actuallyautistic is a great starter hashtag to look for). Watch youtube videos by autistic individuals. Watch shows that center neurodiverse story lines (my board interns all say *Love on the Spectrum* has been the most helpful to them).

Is self-diagnosis valid?

I can see why it's appealing to try and diagnose autism in yourself. If this is something that you are seriously considering, you may think about being evaluated by a professional psychiatrist, if you can. That is, assuming that you think diagnosis would help your situation. Many autistics choose to exist under the radar and self-manage our symptoms. At the same time, knowing what is going on definitively with your neurology can offer a proper roadmap to being successful. In many cases, when parents discover their children are autistic, they shelter and coddle them which inevitably does not prepare them for a lifetime of success.

If you can swing it, nothing beats a diagnosis for getting to the bottom of things and turning difficulties into a road map for overcoming them and finding success. You are on the cusp of something and you may be correct, but it's important to look past your struggles, and work thoughtfully toward your goals and needs.

In many places, in order to get an autism diagnosis you would go to a specialist who performs an hours-long interview, observing for various symptoms and comparing this against the traits in the DSM-5. Once enough information has been recorded, the doctor presents a diagnosis—of autism, something else, or nothing at all. Of course, this diagnostic process is subjective and based on the biases and perception of psychologists, who tend to view autism through a patriarchal lens. Doctors still observe for traditionally male traits, like monologuing over others and blustering through situations. Women, trans people, and genders not socialized as male tend to develop different protective mechanisms to survive and blend in. For example, they might appear quiet, reserved, or shy rather than confident and assertive. Similarly, most diagnostic criteria are intended for children, and adults tend to blur and blend these behaviors. This can make it hard to get a correct diagnosis.

The autistic manner of processing trauma often results in co-occurring mental health conditions and strange coping mechanisms. So as we age and attempt to fit in, we mask so many of our symptoms of autism, making it harder to diagnose. When I was diagnosed at 32, I told the doctor that I was bullied as a child. I told him that I used to speak only in monotone, and that I had learned to do otherwise. Rather than anything about how I present myself today, these two details are what most convinced him. In a diagnostic interview very different from mine, a friend's eight-year-old daughter was not diagnosed because she complimented the interviewer's earrings. The fact that this was a learned (and gendered) habit, not a natural one, was not taken into account because the interviewer's assumption is that autistic people exist in a bubble, would not be able to learn social skills, and wouldn't be thoughtful to communicate in that way. In reality, we are a product of our environment and experiences—just much more intensively so. The child had been taught a gendered survival mechanism of making people like you by giving them compliments.

For many autists, diagnosis becomes even more difficult based on their resource access and where they live. In many places, you'd have to travel hundreds of miles and pay tens of thousands of dollars to get diagnosed. This is further complicated as you age, mask your symptoms, and autism becomes encircled in depression, anxiety, and trauma. So some autistic people make this determination for themselves based on their experience or through realization when their children are diagnosed. And that's at their discretion. The important thing is understanding yourself and how your brain and behavioral traits affect your own path to your own definition of success.

Is the huge increase in autism in the last several decades just due to over-diagnosis and if not, what are the causes and implications?

Even though autistic people have likely been around for many millennia, the first formal diagnoses were in the 1940s. Since then, more and more children and adults worldwide have been diagnosed every year, so much so that some call it an epidemic, and posit goofy explanations for it like vaccines causing autism. In reality, it's simply society and modern medicine catching up to reality.

And the increase in the number of people receiving samesaid diagnosis has gone up, not because the rates of autism are increasing at warp speed, but because we are getting better at recognizing autism for what it is.[12] The news was full of Chicken Little type reporting in 2014, when the autism diagnosis rate jumped from 1 in 88 to 1 in 68. Was it a new vaccine on the market? Nope, we just got an updated diagnostic manual which better defined autism (and its new sister definition, social communication disorder).

The book *NeuroTribes* outlines why so many people who had obvious symptoms of autism were not diagnosed for decades due to the way that disability has been stigmatized after the Holocaust's "cleansing" and lingering ideas spawned from Nazi eugenics.[13] Keep in mind that the last legal forced sterilization of a fellow human being in the United States happened in Oregon in 1981. That's not a typo. The authors of this book were alive then. You may have been, too.

So it's not that there's more autism or overdiagnosis or even a new cause; we are just in a place now where psychology is comfortable calling autism what it is. Also? We are much better

12 The endless claims that autism rates are increasing is demonstrably false. There were always autistic people. We just didn't call them that. And looking back through history it's rather clear that many inventors were autistic. Check out Joe's zine *Autism Causes Vaccines: Stories of Neurodiverse Inventors and Discoveries* and think about traits in people from your own family from several generations ago, before good diagnostic tools. You can't armchair diagnose people, but you can recognize the lineage and behaviors.

13 Side history note. Nazi eugenics are actually American eugenics. As hinted at in an earlier footnote, Hitler was a huge fan of American racist piece of shit Madison Grant and based his whole ethic cleansing mass-murder campaign on Grant's work. If you're into this kind of history, Faith highly recommends the book *Gods of the Upper Air* by Charles King.

at diagnosing it. The term "differential diagnosis" refers to just that: differentiating between diagnoses when there are similar features to consider. Autism shares traits with other mental health diagnoses and was incredibly misunderstood for so long. Imagine that 1 in 45[14] people were misdiagnosed or just deemed quirky for most of the past 500 years. They lived under the surface of society and were treated as uncooperative and difficult. Then think about how diagnosis allows for awareness and acceptance to the ends of allowing people to be a part of society.

How do I know if my autism is mild or if I'm just high-functioning?

Joe'll take this one. There's a running joke in autistic circles, "Is your autism mild or spicy today?" You have likely heard terms like "low functioning autistic" and "high functioning autistic." In addition to being ableist and supremacist, these "functioning labels" are subjective and misleading. The myth of "high" and "low" functioning autistics are concepts built from neurotypical norms and expectations. Essentially, we are judged by how well we mask our behavior to resemble that of a neurotypical. If we can hide our natural ways of expressing ourselves, we are said to be "high functioning." If we cannot pass as neurotypical, we are said to be "low functioning."

---

14 That's a big number to drop without context. 1 in 45 is the CDC's best estimate for the number of autistic individuals of any age in the U.S. Their estimate for children is 1 in 44. The World Health Organization says that among children worldwide, it's probably about 1 in 100.

Has developed a set of healthy coping skills

Can endure stressful situations sometimes. Deemed "high functioning"

Not managing maladaptive responses to trauma and abuse

Remember, autism affects different people in different ways in different situations at different times with differing impacts. Labeling someone as "low functioning" almost universally results in them being segregated from society. Just like labeling someone as "high functioning" results in their autism being put in question and denied. Typically, when someone is deemed "high functioning" it results in them not getting the accommodations that they need and the label ignores the fact that they are almost guaranteed to be trying their hardest to appear neurotypical, or "masking." The ability of an autistic person to function is like anyone else—based on effective coping skills and the confidence to deal with adversity.

Faith jumping in here: Even the DSM-5, which everyone has plenty of grumpies about, doesn't use these terms. When it comes to autism, the DSM-5 requires that a clinician specify the individual's level of support needs. Level 1 is "requiring support," Level 2 is "requiring substantial support," and Level 3 is "requiring very substantial support." And the support levels are based both on social communication disconnections and restricted, repetitive behavior patterns impacting daily activities. The levels aren't about your fundamental abilities or identity. To use a less loaded example, Faith, being middle aged, needs reading glasses. Only for reading. So if she is driving, she needs no support. For close-up activities, she's a Level 2 without the glasses that are on top of her head all the damn time. It's no big deal if she has her glasses. If she doesn't have them, she's going to get frustrated and dysregulated pretty quickly and you're going to have to help a prima out.

Back to Joe. So you can imagine how, situationally, some autistics spend more time on one end of the spectrum than the other. Think of a venn diagram of ability to access coping skills and the trauma and abuse that an autistic person has suffered making it difficult to access those coping skills. When we cannot access our coping skills for long enough, we shut down or have a meltdown.

Similarly, you'll see a lot of discussion about non-speaking autistic people. I didn't speak throughout grade school or for days after watching *Bowling for Columbine*. As in, I could not say a single word for days. I was termed "shy" and my teachers would often try to shame me for using as few words as possible. I responded by refusing to talk whatsoever to people who were disrespectful towards me, which soon became just about everyone in my life. Like many autistic people, I became "non-speaking." I was incapacitated. I was traumatized. I didn't have advocates anywhere in my life. Nobody could see what the problem was, not even me.

With proper respect and agency, this is all preventable. This is why some autistic kids, although they are able to go to college, drive a car, live independently, keep a job, and maintain a relationship, will still fumble and struggle when the cruel stimulus of the sun overwhelms us. Similarly, it's hard to be motivated when you meet difficult and confusing encounters at every turn.

Is it possible for autism to go undiagnosed until your teens or even adulthood?

Of course! It is very possible for you to live into your teens or much longer—even your entire life—without anyone pulling you aside and diagnosing you. I (Joe) wasn't diagnosed until 32! And there were tens of thousands of years before autism was understood where many people were never diagnosed.

When you are a teenager, things are probably coming into focus as you can contrast your own behavior with that of your peers. But being a teenager is to be self-conscious and to feel like you don't fit in; just as it is to be autistic. Teenagers can also be notoriously terrible to each other.

When you know that you are different and almost always made to feel "wrong" or "lesser" in daily life, you lack confidence. Lacking confidence, it's easy to quickly fall into a downward spiral of depression. I cannot tell you how often others would try to "help" me by taking some aspect of something that I had said out of context and lecturing me on how to behave or characterizing my behavior. Inconvenient facts were ignored and narratives were painted. It felt absurd. An important part of diagnosis was realizing that I get to set the parameters of my own life, including who I keep close to me, and how I allow myself to be treated.

It's like the autistic diagnostic criteria joke "five savants and I'm broke." I had so many talents but just kept ending up trusting people that harmed me in the end and took the meager things that I had created. This is a very common story among hundreds of autistic people that I've talked to because we are "difficult" and perhaps, on some level, people see the opportunity to dominate us in this way. While I do think that all of these things are a product of autism, I think that it's fairly clear that dominant culture's influence is what enabled these things to happen unchecked for so many decades.

Diagnosis is the road map to three things:

- Getting along better with others in a substantial and meaningful way, creating healthy and lasting relationships.

- Developing boundaries for yourself so that you can no longer be taken advantage of so easily.

- Surrounding yourself with people who have talents in the areas that you lack or need so that you don't need to learn to excel at things that you aren't predisposed towards and could instead focus on your savant areas.

For me, diagnosis offered instant improvement in all three areas. By understanding what was going on, I suddenly had a frame of reference to make better decisions, know who I wanted and deserved to be around me, and to grow into the person that I wanted to be.

WHAT OTHER CONDITIONS OFTEN OCCUR WITH AUTISM?

What other diagnoses frequently co-occur with autism?

The Netflix television show *Atypical* depicts Sam, an eighteen year old kid in high school. Sam has a supportive family and counselors who help him manage his autism. Sam has a therapist who appears to understand him and charts his progress. Even his bus driver is sympathetic. None of this is realistic, but that's not the point. I (Joe) believe it was an intelligent choice to depict Sam as the anomaly autistic kid with a supportive environment, because it isolates and demonstrates Sam's autism without what most of us experience as autism: co-occurring issues.

Here is a descriptive stats drop by Faith to back Joe up. Co-occuring mental health issues, meaning more than one condition existing in the same body at the same time, are high among autistic people. Approximately 70% of ASD individuals meet diagnostic criteria for at least one co-occuring mental health condition, and 41% experience two or more, anxiety and depression being the most prevalent of these. ADHD (another form of neurodiversity), intellectual disabilities, and learning disabilities are also common. Other common related issues include epilepsy, sleep problems, and gastro-intestinal problems.

The nature of ASD itself, as well as the common co-occurring issues, leads to deep misunderstanding and mistreatment. Those high rates of depression and anxiety aren't a natural result of autism. In fact, they're typically attributed to considerable social isolation and other forms of trauma.

When I (Joe) biked that bookshelf to work in the beginning of this book, I had to lift it over the porch railing, as it was the only way to make the geometry work to get it into the door. Witnessing and empathically relating to my struggle, two strong women walked up and did the heavy lifting for me. It was an awesome moment where I had the rare experience of feeling like I was part of a community. Much more common is the experience of having a meltdown and everyone just ignoring what's happening and not even trying to help.

My partner recently related to me a story about seeing a man in the throes of a neurodivergent meltdown in public, overwhelmed and running back and forth into the street. When another onlooker laughed at the person's misery, my partner suggested that the person was severely overwhelmed and needed help. The onlooker merely shifted his gaze from mocking one stranger's misery to staring at my partner, confused. What would the world look like with awareness about these issues and how to be an ally?

What is the difference between these two scenarios? In the former, it's a relatable experience. Everyone has struggled to move heavy furniture into a narrow doorway. In the latter, the situation is "otherized." Someone having a meltdown or

WHAT WE SHARE IN COMMON

Eliot Daughtry

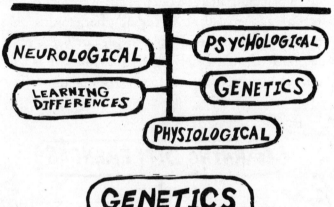

- NEUROLOGICAL
- PSYCHOLOGICAL
- LEARNING DIFFERENCES
- GENETICS
- PHYSIOLOGICAL

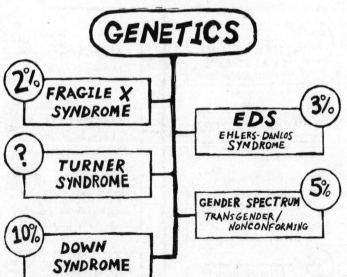

GENETICS

- 2% FRAGILE X SYNDROME
- 3% EDS EHLERS-DANLOS SYNDROME
- ? TURNER SYNDROME
- 5% GENDER SPECTRUM TRANSGENDER/NONCONFORMING
- 10% DOWN SYNDROME

mental health crisis is not seen as relatable. The situation is viewed with judgment, fear, or even scorn.

Due mostly to neurophobia and how others perceive expressions of autism, autistic people are much more likely to experience different forms of trauma. These traumatic events remain unhealed and often result in anxiety, depression, addiction, and maladaptive coping mechanisms that are harmful to others in an attempt to get our needs met. As a result, much of what society thinks of as "autism" is actually a product of how we are treated *because* of our autism.

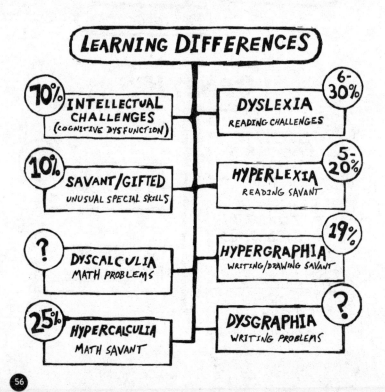

LEARNING DIFFERENCES

70% INTELLECTUAL CHALLENGES (COGNITIVE DYSFUNCTION)

6-30% DYSLEXIA READING CHALLENGES

10% SAVANT/GIFTED UNUSUAL SPECIAL SKILLS

5-20% HYPERLEXIA READING SAVANT

? DYSCALCULIA MATH PROBLEMS

19% HYPERGRAPHIA WRITING/DRAWING SAVANT

25% HYPERCALCULIA MATH SAVANT

? DYSGRAPHIA WRITING PROBLEMS

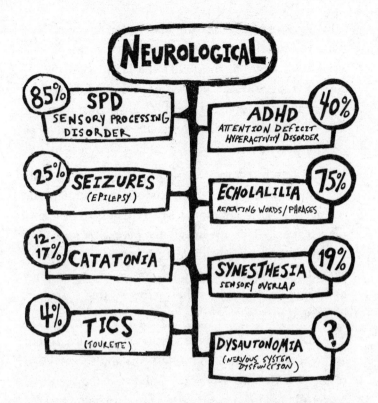

- Autistic children are far more likely than the general population to be violently abused by a parent, guardian, or person responsible for their care. I (Joe) was beaten brutally as far back as my earliest memories until I ran away as a teenager. Many of us don't make it out alive.

- Parents frequently describe having an autistic child as the most traumatic thing that ever happened to them. These feelings are often taken out on the child. Even if that is not the intent, it is frequently the impact. According to autistic philosopher Jim Sinclair, "Non-autistic people see autism as a great tragedy, and parents experience continuing disappointment and grief at all stages of the child's and family's life cycle." Most parents have an idea of who their child will be that is an impossible standard for anyone to recreate. The child comes out being exactly who *they are*. The task, as parents, is to love and care for that person.

- I (Joe) often feel myself being identified as vulnerable or prey; someone who is easy to manipulate by strangers and acquaintances. My weakness is somehow perceivable. This results in people frequently attempting to pressure me into having sex, taking advantage of me, attempting to obtain my belongings or money by force, or other activities that I am not interested in.

- The manifestations of these feelings result in treatment and a trajectory that continues into adulthood. As a result of a lifetime of violence, abuse, being seen as a regretful pain in someone else's life, and being treated as vulnerable prey, autistic people face extremely high rates of mental problems, such as anxiety, depression, self-harm, and addiction. Autistic people of all ages are victims of violence at much higher rates than the general population.

- Our life expectancy is only 36 years. One principal cause of this is suicide (see the 2018 study by Culpin et. al. in the references). In fact, suicide is the leading cause of death for autistic people. We give up after

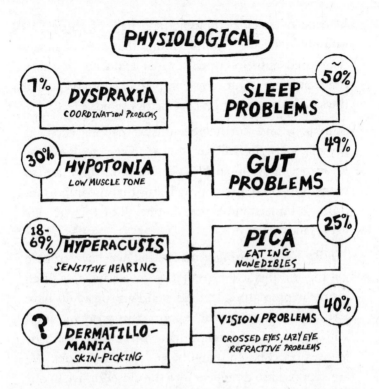

being treated this way. Even 14% of autistic children experience suicidal thoughts. I (Joe) know that I did, from a very young age. Compare that to 0.5% of the general population and you'll begin to understand the nature of the problem.

- Autistic people tend to be more honest in reporting our feelings of suicidal ideation while other populations tend to lie about it. As a result, it's hard to obtain clear statistics unless people are successful. Still, one study found that two thirds of autistic adults had a lifetime of suicidal thoughts and half of those had attempted suicide. Another found that 66% of newly diagnosed autistics were suicidal and half of those made attempts. Our rates compare to those of people physically dependent on cocaine or opioids.

- Stubborn and fortunate autistic people such as myself, who survive past 36, are likely to have the life expectancy of an NT person. Still, there are so many unnatural, premature deaths that the important thing to understand is that despite all of this, our life expectancy is 36.

- "Difficulty socializing" means that we have trouble getting the medical care that we need and this often results in premature death as well. Autistic adults have virtually no institutional support. Every organization with any kind of funding that you've ever heard of focuses on children, parents, and/or counselors. We are supposed to disappear into the closet or live in our parents' basement.

- Estimating the unemployment rate for autistic adults is difficult, the numbers vary wildly . . . from 20% to 85% (with the higher numbers being far more likely). This erodes our self-worth in a capitalist society. In my Autistic Support Action Network (ASAN) group, this statistic is mirrored exactly. As a result, we are much more likely to be homeless, as I have been as well. Homelessness creates a further multiplier for mental illness, addiction, and being violently victimized.

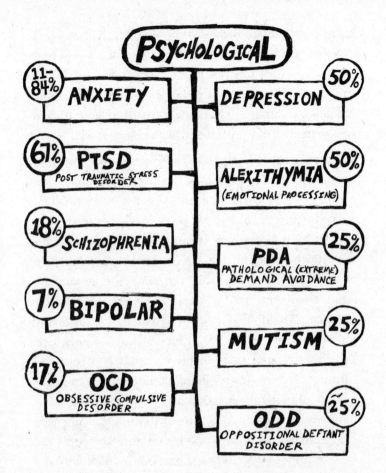

PSYCHOLOGICAL

ANXIETY 11-84%

DEPRESSION 50%

PTSD 67%
POST TRAUMATIC STRESS DISORDER

ALEXITHYMIA 50%
(EMOTIONAL PROCESSING)

SCHIZOPHRENIA 18%

PDA 25%
PATHOLOGICAL (EXTREME) DEMAND AVOIDANCE

BIPOLAR 7%

MUTISM 25%

OCD 17%
OBSESSIVE COMPULSIVE DISORDER

ODD ~25%
OPPOSITIONAL DEFIANT DISORDER

- We experience very high rates of digestive problems and epilepsy, likely from the increased cognitive load. Best guess as to why? The tenth cranial nerve carries information and inflammation to every bodily system and major organ, including the brain. Problems in one area spread like wildfire throughout the body. As you might imagine by now, it's difficult to determine if autistic people are prone to these issues, if they are a product of a brain that operates at an entirely different level, or if they are results of being underserved by the medical system. Correlation doesn't determine causality, which is to say, the whole system is so fucked up we really can't say where the problem starts.

- We are far more likely than the general population to be shot by police. You may have seen the 2016 high profile case in Florida where a 26-year-old autistic man, Arnaldo Rios Soto, and his behavioral therapist were shot at by police when Arnaldo was playing with his favorite toy truck in the street. Arnaldo's experience is a much more probable outcome for an autistic adult than Sam is on *Atypical*. Despite supportive parents, Arnaldo has been mistreated institutionally for almost his entire life, which created a series of behaviors related to both his isolation and repeated trauma. The podcast *AfterEffect* does a magnificent job of humanizing Arnaldo and demonstrating what happens to autistic adults in institutions. One thing that it's important to understand is that autistic people are shot by police frequently because our mannerisms and behaviors are interpreted as raising a flag, not because we are violent or uncooperative. Autistic people often do not understand social expectations in an encounter with police or simply don't respond fast enough. Police are usually not trained to interact with autistic people and we provoke their fight response out of fear. I have lost count how many times I've been harassed by the police for being odd. In one case an officer pulled me over on my bike because a house had been robbed in the direction that I was coming from. I explained the math of the trajectory to him and that I couldn't be the suspect because I would have broken the land speed record to have made it as far as I did. He responded with "I'm just doing my job. Don't be so annoyed." I wasn't annoyed; I was countering his suspicions with facts. It might sound snotty to say I know I'm lucky to be alive, but it's also true. And there would likely be no repercussions if a police officer killed me. Jonathon Aledda, the officer who shot and wounded Arnaldo's therapist, which resulted in Arnaldo becoming evicted from his group home, was initially found guilty of culpable negligence, but his conviction was overturned in 2022.

What's the connection between autism and trauma?

Faith here. Autistic individuals are far more likely to experience adverse events and traumatic experiences, while also less likely to be diagnosed or treated for the traumatic stress they experience. Interestingly, it isn't solely trauma perpetuated upon the autistic individual because they are easier to victimize; population data demonstrates that autistic children are also exposed to significantly more trauma in the form of familial divorce, parents with substance use problems and/or mental illness, neighborhood violence, and poverty. Since correlation is not causality, we can't really posit a guess as to why this is the case. Quite likely there is no singular origin story to why these numbers are so high.

So when we discuss the high instances of depression and anxiety among autistic people, we also have to factor in the significant role that traumatic stress may be playing in developing these conditions. One study demonstrated that 90% of individuals diagnosed with both ASD and a mood disorder had a significant trauma history. And of the autistic individuals with no co-occurring mood disorder, only 40% had a trauma history.

If you've read other things Faith has written, you're full up on how trauma changes the brain and body. If you have somehow managed to avoid her nonsense,[15] here's a super quick overview. Traumatic stress, a trauma response, or full-blown PTSD is what happens when a traumatic experience overwhelms our ability to cope.

The human brain is a storytelling machine whose job it is to make sense of the world. The mechanism by which we make sense of the world is different for everyone. Understanding someone else's sense-making is called an *enactive approach*. So let's use an enactive approach to understand how trauma works when you are autistic. The three features of the brain that likely play the biggest role in why an autistic person is more susceptible to trauma reactions are: a lower neurological threshold, differences in ability to self-regulate, and differences in sense-making. Let's talk about what all these things mean, specifically in relation to adverse events.

15 *Unfuck Your Brain: Using Science to Get Over Anxiety, Depression, Anger, Freak-outs, and Triggers* (2016, Microcosm Publishing)

Neurological threshold is the term used to describe the limits of a human being's ability to process/tolerate sensory stimuli. We each have a threshold of information our bodies can take in through the senses. There are only a certain amount of sounds in our ears, sights in our range of vision, smells, temperature changes, or things on our skin that we can handle without becoming overwhelmed. Autistic individuals tend to have a lower neurological threshold than allistics, at least in some areas. While more of some sensory stimuli may be soothing (a weighted blanket, thumping bass music), those sensations are being used to block out other sensations or calm a nervous system that has become overloaded from other input.

Self-regulation and sense-making are exactly what they sound like: Our ability to moderate our nervous systems in any given situation (especially difficult ones) and our ability to make sense of the world. These are skills that are partially innate in humans and are learned and curated further as we mature and grow. These systems work differently among neurodivergent people. And it isn't just as simple an answer as *it's harder.* The fact that *it's different* is enough. If the allistics around you have an agreed-upon, shared reality of an event and you don't see it that way? You now may feel confused, rejected, anxious, isolated, detached, and questioning everything about yourself as a person.

If our trauma responses are more about how we process a traumatic event and the support we have in healing and recovery (or lack thereof), it then entirely makes sense that an autistic person would be more susceptible to traumatic stress. Both from things that everyone would agree are traumatic and from things that many people wouldn't necessarily perceive as traumatic. One study surveyed autistic people, assessing them both for what the APA's 5th edition of the Diagnostic and Statistical Manual (DSM-5) considers a trauma that results in PTSD and what autistic people found to be traumatic. The answers were heartbreaking. Many people struggled with bullying, abandonment by family members, grief, their own mental health struggles, and the ASD diagnostic process itself.

And now that we have some better understanding of how an autistic person sees the world (enactive approach) it becomes very obvious why these issues could easily be perceived as traumatic stress. And if you don't have the support you need, this can turn into PTSD. I have had shitty therapists myself over the years. It doesn't feel good, but it never took terribly long to process through to *"Well, fuck them, then . . . this is not for me."* But if you are autistic and you are being told constantly that you are the one getting everything wrong? Especially if you are a kiddo who already struggles to communicate and you're being forced through this process? And you internalize all these disconnections and communication problems as the responsibility of your being? Traumatic as fuck.

How do autistics experience and overcome trauma?

Joe here. I always assumed that trauma played out similarly for me as it does for most people. In the past year, talking about it openly with allistic people, I came to realize how different things are for us.

I have a particular chair that is an important part of my morning routine.

Once, while sitting in that chair, I received a piece of horrible news. The experience of receiving that news was so tied to that chair that I couldn't separate the two. The trauma became so deeply associated with the physical chair that every time I sat in it, I would experience it again and again. I've had similar experiences with rooms, smells, blankets, tastes, and sounds.

I had to get rid of that chair immediately or experience those same feelings over and over. I'm fortunate to have done the personal work to have built a self-image where I found a partner who respects me and to believe that I am *worth* not feeling that way again and again. My partner understands the gravity of requests like "We need to get rid of this chair and go find a new one today." She dropped what she was doing that night and we took a walk together to find a new one. It was salvation; a pilgrimage of sorts. The new chair renewed my ritual and routines.

For most of my life I have not had this kind of understanding or support. I have struggled with basic tasks like feeding and taking care of myself. Often, my focus and emotional state were wildly distracting from my goals, meaning, and purpose. And when a therapist asked me to envision myself in a safe place, I realized that none had existed throughout the first 32 years of my life.

Everywhere that I've found myself has proven to be remarkably unsafe. Growing up, I was frequently beaten and ridiculed for doing what I intended as empathic, selfless acts for other people's benefit. At school I was teased and hit for offenses ranging from wearing the wrong pants to hanging out with the wrong people to enjoying the wrong hobbies. Left to my own devices in the city, I lacked the ability to determine when I was entering an unsafe situation or when a stranger had dubious motives in engaging with me. In intimate situations, I lacked the sense to understand that I could advocate for what I needed, wanted, and enjoyed. I had been told so many times that my own lack of interest in sex wasn't a factor to be considered and that I should go along with what the other person wanted. I've come to realize that I am only interested in sexual and romantic partners where there is a high level of prior mutual emotional investment. But I stuck around for two years in one relationship where my wants were dictated to me and my needs were denied. I was told what clothes I was allowed to wear and that when my partner was jealous, it was my fault. I fled that relationship to a life of homelessness, and from there I gradually built the life that I have today. Reviewing my life in this way after an ongoing campaign to actively harm me, it's clear why I never felt safe until I was 43. It took over ten years of being in a healthy relationship, living in a safe home, having my needs met, and less frequent threats and attacks on my well-being.

Prior to turning 43, I had the realization that, like my service dog, the one place where I feel safe in the world is on Amtrak trains. It's a tender mix of predictability, consistency, and familiarity. Even the things that are inconsistent are consistently inconsistent. I know what to pack to have a positive trip. I know that my train is going to be late and what to do when it is. I know that I am more functional in that environment than most people, which gives me a bit of an edge over neurotypicals who normally have a bit of an edge over me.

I know that I will be able to get writing done and that no one will interrupt me. I know that I will be inspired because I will have an adequately protected environment and thus adequate space in my brain to notice things. I know that, above all, my routines will be respected and honored and no one will attempt to overwrite my experience or dictate what I want or need. In this way, I find safety. I have a little bubble around me and I know that spending days in transit will be some of the most joyous in my life.

Sometimes, thinking about our problems in a new environment can be helpful from decoupling trauma. Recently, I've been reading about the brain science of travel and how different environments jog your brain in different ways. Everything from different smells, sounds, sights, and interactional dynamics make our brains interface differently with the same problems. We literally think differently and solve problems in new ways in different environments. This seems to be why most people go on vacation; to get a break of reprieve from their usual routine and better understand their daily life. I find vacation tremendously stressful but even traveling for work is a huge relaxation because it helps me to think about and solve problems in a more effective manner. In this manner, travel can be a vacation for the brain from stress.

No offense or whatever, but I'm not even sure if it's autism, trauma, or both.

None taken! Very good question! A trauma response can look like autism, especially in younger humans. We don't suggest trying to unravel these differentials on your own, but to see a professional who specializes in this work. A good one will consult with colleagues in the field with an eye to discernment to ensure clinical consensus. But to help the process, three specialists in the field (Drs. Katherine Kuhl-Meltzoff Stavropoulos, Yasamine Bolourian, and Jan Blacher) created a graphic to help explain both the differences and the overlap. They also made their work available under creative commons so we can share it with you. Check it out on the next page.

Are autistic people at higher risk of suicide? How can I help?

Short answer? Yes. And with the caveat that it isn't because autism itself makes you suicidal. Just like with other high risk groups, suicidality isn't about wanting to be dead. It's about wanting the pain of our living circumstances to stop. And we see no other way of making that happen unless we cease to exist.

Autism Spectrum Disorder (ASD) individuals are at a significantly higher risk than the general population of suicidal thoughts and behaviors (meaning ideation/plans/attempts/dying by suicide). Suicide is the leading cause of premature death among autistic people, and this extends to children and youth, not just adults. One in four autistic youth experience

Autism Spectrum Disorder

Post-Traumatic Stress Disorder

Deficits in social-emotional reciprocity

Lack of interest in peers

Social withdrawal

Deficits in social-communication

Failure to share emotions/affect

Reduction of positive emotions

Repetitive use of objects

Repetitive Play

Intrusive memories

Inflexible adherence to routines/insistence on sameness

Outbursts

Irritability/Anger

Associated feature of Autism Spectrum Disorder

Sleep Difficulty

Recurrent nightmares/difficulty falling or staying asleep

Diagram of symptom overlap in ASD and PTSD (re-printed from Stavropoulos et al., 2018 under the terms and conditions of the Creative Commons Attribution (CC BY) license (creativecommons.org/licenses/by/4.0/)).

suicidal ideation and almost one in ten attempt suicide. Autistic youth are six times more likely to attempt suicide and twice more likely to die by suicide than the general population.[16] The question, then, becomes: is the increase in suicidality related to the mental health issues or the neurodivergence?

The answer is that certain mental health issues frequently experienced by autistic individuals—specifically mood disorders, thought disorders, and PTSD—are associated with an increase in suicidality, while others (such as anxiety) are not. This seems similar to the rest of the population, however the rates of suicidality are still higher among autistic individuals than their allistic peers, even when mental health issues are specifically controlled for in the research. Meaning someone who is neuronormative and depressed is at higher risk than your regular average human (do those exist anymore?), but someone who is neurodivergent and depressed has *much* higher risk.

With these numbers being so high, you would think that clinicians would get lots of grad school and CE training on screening for suicidality, especially when working with individuals who are historically at much higher risk. However, researchers demonstrate repeatedly that therapists and other clinical treatment providers do not feel confident in our ability to screen for suicidality with autistic clients, which means no appropriate care through safety planning.

---

16 Researchers in the past two decades have published findings in gold standard medical journals such as JAMA that demonstrate over and over that most autistic people meet criteria for at least one mental health issue.

And while no human (clinician or otherwise) gets things perfect, even among those of us who are trying and do have some understanding of what neurodivergence looks like? Researchers have also found that clinicians struggle to parse out suicidality and stimming behavior. Because so many autistic individuals engage in stimming (the fancy term for that is neurodivergence-related restricted repetitive behaviors, or RRBs) and that those behaviors can be self-harming, clinicians and other care-takers can mistake suicidality for stimming.

For example, someone running into traffic is definitely a behavior that anyone with a heart/soul/brain will be worried about. Now imagine, if an autistic person did so with the absolute intent to be hit by a car and killed. But everyone around them said *"Oh, well. Stan gets overwhelmed and runs off when that happens. Let's add an anxiety med and mood stabilizer to help with autistic overwhelm."* No safety planning, no discourse, no plan to deal with the real underlying issue. And now Stan, already suicidal and thwarted in his first attempt, now has two new big bottles of pills to simplify finishing the job.

And yes, suicidality is incredibly difficult to predict. We can see the trail that got someone there in hindsight, but even the best clinician misses things in the moment. So how do we minimize the chance of missing these clues that something is wrong? Just like every toddler should have an M-CHAT-R screening, everyone receiving healthcare services should be screened for suicidality and assisted with safety planning.

Researchers have found that more than half of people who die by suicide had visited a healthcare provider within one month of their death. So the Joint Commission (JCHAO), a nonprofit accreditation board for U.S. hospitals, recommended in 2016 that hospitals should screen all clients for suicide risk, regardless of the reason for their visit. Hard agree, whether someone is in the hospital or not. All health care providers should assess everyone. If you have ever been my intern you heard this all the time, and now the people who are reading this book are hearing it, too. Everyone gets screened for suicidality and everyone gets a crisis plan, no matter what.

The National Institute for Mental Health has developed a quick screening tool that can be used by any healthcare professional, even those who know very little about mental health and/or autism. It wasn't designed with neurodiversity in mind, but researchers have found that it is simple enough that it's still an appropriate and effective tool, and it's been implemented in clinics that focus on working with autistic people. Great start.

If you're a medical provider who wants to do a more comprehensive assessment, any tool you are using to assess suicidality risk can be augmented. While the NIMH tool is super pragmatic and easy to use, many of us are looking for other risk indicators when doing suicide assessments and safety planning and support of others. The higher risk and specific needs of autistic individuals led me to do a similar research review, and I found some really interesting data points. For example, neither the level of support that the individual needs nor their IQ had any impact on the frequency of suicidality. Gender also washed out as an indicator once meta analytic reviews were compiled. But some data points became very important very quickly.

So what does matter? I came up with the mnemonic ASD CARES to help remember specific risk factors and care needs for autistic individuals:

- **Age is greater than 10:** While among the general population, the risk of sucide does not emerge until someone is a teenager, it happens much earlier among ASD individuals. Suicidality starts to be expressed in children as young as preschool age and research shows the chances of it being acted upon gets really high by age 10.

- **Sexual abuse:** While all forms of abuse are associated with risk, sexual abuse is signficantly higher, especially when the offense was recent.

- **Difficulties with social communication/isolation/ loneliness:** Just because someone with ASD may struggle to make and maintain relationships doesn't mean they don't want or need them. Loneliness is a huge issue among autistic individuals and a huge risk factor for suicidality.

- **Camouflaging/masking:** The stress of trying to "act normal" (compensatory strategies used to "hide" one's autism). Masking is also often taught as part of applied behavioral analysis, even though it operates as such a stressor that it becomes a trigger for suicidality.

- **ACEs/traumatic stress/PTSD:** Adverse childhood events (traumatic experiences), traumatic stress experienced at any age, and fully-realized PTSD are especially difficult for autistic individuals to manage and recover from and which can operate as a trigger for suicidality.

- **Resource availability (SES/location):** Lower socioeconomic status and/or living in a rural area which often equal less access to appropriate resources and care acts as a stressor which leads to increased suicidality.

- **Ethnic minority (Black/Hispanic specifically):** Among the general population in the U.S., white individuals are more likely to die by suicide, but among autistic people, the numbers are highest among Black and Hispanic individuals over white and Asian individuals. The research did not indicate numbers for Indigenous or South Asian peoples, though we would encourage including them as higher risk as a ethnic minority until different data proves otherwise.

- **Non-cis:** While rates of suicidality are high among non-cis individuals (transgender, nonbinary, or agender), the rates are even higher if the individual is also autistic.

- **Existing mood or thought disorder:** This is one of the bigger indicators. In suicide scale parlance, it's a "red flag" requiring a more complex safety plan. Other common co-occuring issues (anxiety and ADHD are two big ones) are not associated with an increase in suicidal ideation, but depression, bipolar disorder, and psychosis risks are even higher among autistic individuals than their counterparts without these diagnostics.

- **Experienced as behaviorally challenging**: An autistic person may struggle with communication but that doesn't mean that they aren't aware of how others perceive them. And those around them do not have to be abusive or unkind to relay that they find them exasperating or exhausting, which can make them think of themselves as unwanted or a drain on resources, which leads to suicidality.

- **Domineered/bullied:** Peer bullying (in-person or cyber) are risk factors, but bullying by adult perpetrators with power are associated with the highest risk level.

- **Schedule disruptions/routine changes (especially those perceived as permanent, such as moving or bereavement):** A need for schedule sameness is a common feature for many autistic people. When that gets disrupted, managing the disruption can be incredibly difficult. When the disruption is going to be or is perceived as life-changing or permanent, it can activate suicidality.

None of these indicators are designed to have you hospitalize your loved one just because they're going through it. They are meant to be things to watch for, just like they are with any other member of society. If a bunch of stuff was going on in their life that made them more at risk, you would keep that in mind, right? You would be asking them up front if they were thinking about suicide, making a safety plan, and getting them into a higher level of care if they were at imminent risk. Same thing here, just some new considerations to keep in mind in the process.

Can therapy help autistic people?

Faith here. Many of us are struggling to keep sane in an insane world. Equally unfortunate is the fact that many of y'all brilliant, funny, smart as fuck neurodivergent (ND)[17] peeps out there think that therapy isn't for you. Maybe you had bad experiences with therapists trying to "fix" you. Or you did your time with behavioral specialists as a kid and you were told that traditional talk therapy was a waste for "your kind." And that's just a steaming pile of bullshit. If *anyone* could benefit from support in navigating living in the upside down, it's you. You have a clearer picture of what's crazy then the rest of us, after all. Therapy can help you process your confusion, frustration, and all of your urgings to ragequit this game. And a therapist who understands the unique coolness of your brain can help you use the things you are best at to not just survive, but to thrive.

A therapist can also give you feedback on how others perceive what's normal for you. Someone who listens and gets who you are, but can say, "Hey, that's the type of interaction

17 Anyone with a brain or neurotype that is not neurotypical, meaning these brain differences affect how their brains work. As a result, they have different strengths and challenges from people whose brains don't have those differences.

that can make it hard to get a job, get a date, make friends, etc." can make a huge difference in your life. It's far better to hear it from someone who digs you and isn't offended by how you roll, but also wants to help you accomplish those goals that require interpersonal interaction (read: all of them).

Search out therapists who are ND-friendly. Ask questions. Try an initial session. Just like you wouldn't wear shoes that give you continuous blisters, find someone who fits. And if therapy isn't your bag, consider neurofeedback,[18] mindfulness meditation, qi gong, or yoga. There are a lot of evidence-based wellness interventions that don't require you spilling your guts in someone's office. Fighting for your own contentment and a meaningful life is the bravest, most powerful thing you can do.

A good therapeutic relationship can be buddhasent for those of you who are neurodivergent. If we ascribe to John Elder Robinson's statement that 99% of the world's problems may not require an autistic brain, but 1% of the problems do, then a therapist's understanding of what makes you special may be lifesaving. You need someone who will be supportive, instead of prescriptive and belittling. I want you to stan on Frida Kahlo, Legos, or particle physics to your heart's content if that's your thing. We need your brain for those 1% of problems. But I also want you to be able to better navigate the overwhelm of the other 99% when a lot of people are going to have no idea where you're coming from, and you've had years or decades of being told you are fundamentally broken or wrong.

---

18 Joe might be the greatest advertisement and advocate for neurofeedback, having been prescribed it for a sleeping problem, and coming out a year later shedding reactions from childhood and adult trauma!

Therapy can also be buddhasent if you have a neurodivergent partner, either for yourself or couples therapy. I get so many referrals for neurologically mixed relationships. Which, in this case, means one partner is neurodivergent and the other one is a boring normie like me. I only very recently found out that I have a reputation for being great at helping establish better communication, boundaries, etc with these partners. But you want to know a secret? I am not doing anything that I don't do with couples that are *both* boring normies. I would say the needs are more pressing and when things don't go well it can be more distressing but the skills are the same. For example asking clearly and concretely for what one wants from a partner, embracing emotional accountability, taking breaks from overwhelming arguments, etc? I encourage every couple (or throuple or any relationship configuration that comes through the door) to speak more plainly and directly, define needs and wants cleanly, and generally stop expecting someone to read your mind just because they love you.

And for you parents of autistic folks? Therapy for you, too! Not because "ugh, you're going to screw up your kid and should pay someone to yell at you," but because we so often focus on the autistic person we lose sight of the fact that the people who are trying so hard to love and nurture and care for them are struggling, too. And they need support, too. It's not fair to ask you to cry quietly in the bathroom with the shower running so no one in your household can hear. You also need consideration, compassion, perspective, and a cozy therapist's office with the really good tissues with the lotion in them if you need to have a solid cry.

WHAT SHOULD EVERYONE KNOW ABOUT AUTISTIC EXPERIENCES?

Why do allistics often infantilize autistics?

The doctor who diagnosed my (Joe's) autism made an offhand remark one day. Noticing that I rode my bicycle to our appointments, he said "Some people might say that there's no point in riding your bike. You can't save the planet from global warming. What would you say to that?" I had read enough psychology to understand that his use of passive verbs was a dog whistle to mean that he felt that way. I responded before sitting down, "I would tell *some people* to research the correlation between divorce rates and duration of car commutes and you'll see that science is pretty sound around this matter."[19] I was already in my 30s at this time. I had weathered many storms and built my confidence up. If I had been younger or less confident in myself, or if my motives in bicycle commuting had actually been to stave off global warming, this would have destroyed me. Why a psychologist who specializes in autistic children would say this to a patient continues to confound me. Instead, I was able to flip the script and have more knowledge about psychology—his own area of supposed specialization. It quickly became our final appointment.

For autistic people, learning how to take care of ourselves is a bit different. We tend to ask a lot of serious questions about things that are obvious to NTs, such as "Why do I need to wash

---

19 "Because I like it" or "Because I want to" are perfectly cromulent answers as well.

my clothes?" or "Why can't I just play video games all day?" As a result, NTs tend to lose patience with us. We take up a lot of emotional and mental space and we often get pushed into the metaphorical closet. We grow up awkwardly with some things worked out and others not. Our emotional age is quite a bit less than our intellectual or human age. The result tends to be that we are very smart but immature and sassy know-it-alls. As a result, we are perceived as being something of a thorny jerk, like we are doing all of this on purpose.

Caretakers, parents, teachers, authority figures, and counselors tend to respond in one of two ways: sheltering and coddling autistics or abusing us. I can intellectually understand both of these responses but they are both equally ineffective at creating the desired outcome. They are either left with a childish, dependent adult who cannot take care of themselves or a resentful adult with a series of maladaptive ways of attempting to get our needs met. Nobody wants this and it's not serving anybody, so a middle ground must be found if we are to become independent, confident adults.

What are common problems adult autistic people face?

Not being able to relate with the people around us. This works both ways: the autistic person cannot understand the values, ideas, and priorities put forward by the people around them and thus cannot engage meaningfully with the people that they encounter on the day to day. And conversely, the autistic person has trouble finding people who are interested in the things they are obsessed with, so they feel alone, and misunderstood, and unappreciated.

The most common problems are near universal:

- Difficulty forming meaningful relationships that are equitable and fulfilling to both parties. This results in anxiety, loneliness, and alienation.

- Difficulty maintaining interest in and understanding rules created by outside parties that do not serve or achieve their stated goals. E.g., the rules do not achieve the results or solve the problems that they set out to but are adhered to anyway.

- Difficulty maintaining an attitude of learned optimism. This is the ability to see one's successes as a result of one's actions rather than a fluke, and seeing one's failures as circumstantial or environmental or to be learned from rather than a state of inevitability.[20]

- Suicide risk is incredibly high, especially as autistics enter adulthood and middle age. See #1.

Can you cure autism? If not, how can I learn to live with the fact that I am autistic?

Joe'll take this one. No, you cannot cure autism, not in the way that you mean. You cannot strip autism from the brain or the person. Even if you were to get a brain transplant or rewire the brain, autism has already informed all of your interactions and

20 For more on this, read Dr. Faith's *Unfuck Your Brain*, which extensively details how to apply learned optimism in your own life.

thought processes, which statistically result in discrimination and the resulting anxiety, depression, trauma, and addiction.

However, you can learn to manage autism and mitigate the negative effects. Again, negative effects are mostly a product of how other people treat autistics.

I'm really sorry to hear that you are having a hard time adjusting to your diagnosis. There is a lot that you can do to live the life that you want. The most important thing is to reject everyone else's expectations and the limitations that they impose upon you. Because the sky's the limit.

Also, I'm not sure how old you are but for whatever reason people stop picking on each other as they get older. It actually makes no sense why people are so mean to each other at younger ages. Society can be really difficult. Don't live by their expectations; live by your rules. For example, I never graduated from college, but I see that as a failing of college, not of myself.

Find your meaning and purpose. Invest deeply in it. Build your life around it. Become an expert in it. Your quirks and oddities will not matter anymore, if anyone even notices them. If you are interested, there are cognitive behavioral therapy (CBT) social skills training that can help you relate to neurotypicals and understand their norms and communication habits. It's learning to speak to imperialists in their native language, and negotiation is a vital part of shifting and toppling empires. It helps you communicate better what you are feeling and experiencing as well. Once you find your meaning and purpose and enmesh yourself in it, people will see your confidence and come to you because you are an expert. They want to know your opinion and it doesn't matter if your brain is like theirs. They desire your expertise and want your help.

Find the people who care about you. They won't always get you but if they are patient and care, it's enough to bring them around to get it eventually. After getting divorced and losing everything, I've been in an awesome relationship for thirteen years with a neurotypical. She doesn't always understand what is going on in my head but when I explain to her, she has the care and patience to respect it. The fascinating thing is that she can advocate much more effectively on my behalf than I can for myself. In turn, I am able to better support her needs, wants, and love languages by telling her how much I see and appreciate this as well as helping to solve objective problems where I am more skilled than her. More people like her are out there, and the longer you're around to meet them, the more people there will be to cherish you. Immerse yourself in people who understand you fundamentally, like the movement-building support group Autism Support Action Network (ASAN) or online networks.

If I need to center myself, I have a few different exercises. For example, when I was nine, I figured out the numerical placement of every letter in the alphabet and created mathematical equations from those letter values. This made algebra very confusing to me later, but it gave me something that I could do anywhere within my own head and without being mocked for stimming. No one could see it or disrupt it or take it away from me. It centered me. Today, I will say my dog's name until I feel better.

Similarly, when other people do things that upset me, I compose a tweet in my head that objectively names and explains how their behavior was inappropriate and hilarious. It offloads the trauma and allows me to move on with my day. I publish the tweets about half of the time when I feel that they would amuse or benefit other people. If it just is going to be interpreted as me complaining, I keep it to myself.

We have a gift for humor so if someone is rude to you, learn how to sass them back. Even if you never have to do it, you'll feel more confident being prepared. Our humor can be sassy humor.

Don't let anyone else tell you what you can or cannot do. Don't see your ASD as a limitation. It's merely one aspect of yourself that informs your personality and character.

It's wrong that this shit is imposed on us. We didn't ask to be born into their world, and neurotypicals need to get their act together too. But that isn't something we can control so we have to start with ourselves, our choices, and building a movement that is strong enough to establish respect.

What is stimming?

Stimming is a coping mechanism that centers a person in their body and reduces stress. It's also called things like "flapping" and can include any behavior ranging from wildly waving to repeating a phrase to just opening and closing the hands. Due to societal stigmatization of stimming, lots of autistic people utilize subtler or more socially acceptable variants, such as drumming on their thighs, playing with their hair, or rocking in place.

When I was a kid, I would rub the skin off the palms of my hands, incessantly chew my nails, or feel the texture of my wet, torn-up, dirty blanket between my thumb and forefinger. Naturally, the first time I was caught by a neighbor doing this, I could no longer deny to myself that I did it. I didn't know why I liked it and studies regarding stimming were virtually nonexistent. I just knew that it was comforting in my small, chaotic world. Naturally, the blanket was destroyed in the washing machine.

There was a fad around autistic people using fidget spinners for this purpose a few years ago. Today, I stim by running my hand through my thinning hair and saying the name of my dog, often to people's confusion.

Again, because stimming is a socially *unacceptable* coping mechanism, lots of parents of autistic people try to eradicate it from their behavior, which is effectively abuse as it is a primary way to comfort ourselves and prevent a meltdown. Essentially, it's yet another aspect of being autistic that requires engaging where you feel capable and educating others about what it is, why we do it, and how its function isn't harming anyone else. Like many things about being autistic, it's just stigmatized.

I'm fairly sure that stimming is the only socially unacceptable coping mechanism. Not convinced? Go to a bar and watch how socially acceptable drinking is. Still not convinced? Go on the Internet and look how much of it is about comforting strangers by saying that some people are "garbage." Consider how all of this coping affects other people and how harmless yet socially unacceptable stimming is.

How can I support my adult sibling who doesn't believe they are autistic?

I (Joe) can see why it's appealing to try and diagnose a loved one, but you really cannot do this. Even if you were a medical expert on autism, you are too close to your sibling to make an objective analysis like this. I understand that you're probably approaching this with the best of intentions and wanting to help, but there are plenty of other reasons that they may exhibit these symptoms and struggles.

If the person in question is interested, nothing beats an actual diagnosis when it comes to getting to the bottom of things and turning difficulties into a road map for overcoming them and finding success, so see above for hints in that direction. You may be correct, but it's more important to work with the individual towards *their* needs and goals than it is to speculate about their diagnosis. They know what's right for them more than you ever could.

In reality, the symptoms of autism and every other mental health problem are often a product of how someone with these conditions is treated. So your solution is simple:

- Do not apply the stigma or diagnosis that you believe applies
- Talk to them about specific behaviors and problems and focus on those

- Create an actionable, step-by-step plan for dealing with the behavior that is straining your relationship

If they are not interested in that after an agreed-upon period of time, explain that you need to withdraw from the relationship for your own health.

That's how you help, by having appropriate boundaries. You can't change other people, only yourself and how you interact with them. Don't write off your sibling's chances of success. Lots of autistics and plain weirdos are super successful. Lack of diagnosis or later diagnosis can also be helpful with proper support for two reasons:

- Without a diagnosis early in life, the autistic person is neither socially segregated nor told that what they can accomplish is limited.

- Because someone has struggled earlier in life, they have less pressure placed on them to fulfill others' expectations.

With proper support and encouragement, the combination of these two factors can lead many autistic people to pursue their own interests to tremendous success. The combination of these tends to result in sufficient freedom to achieve their meaning and purpose. In many ways, the autistic traits can help to guide each person's path.

For example, being thought of as weird and stubborn was tough on friendships, situations, and relationships, but didn't hurt how I was perceived as a business owner. In fact, being considered a stubborn asshole is an expected quality in CEOs. However, once I understood what was going on, I didn't want to be thought of this way, and diagnosis helped me to reframe this in my own mind, understand my needs, and even to change my behavior. So while this road was very bumpy, it's far preferable to being insulated from failures or being further socially isolated than I already am. Similarly, this offers many lessons for how to ensure their success:

1) Listen and accept people just the way they are. This will improve their self-esteem and confidence. Offer compliments on things that are real and tangible, but don't make shit up. We know when we are being placated.

2) Don't try to hold them up to the same standards that you would a neurotypical of the same age. Their life is different and so is their brain at every level. This is especially important for kiddos, teens, and adults in their twenties. The prefrontal cortex doesn't finish developing until our mid-to-late twenties. Neurodiversity expert Russell Barkley states that there is often a three-year lag between chronological age and developmental age in many areas for Austic and ADHD people. An autistic fifteen year old may be fire on the debate team and so ahead in coursework they are going to graduate high school early.... but have the interest in dating of a twelve-year-old. Everyone develops differently, and that is especially true for autistic individuals.

3) Spend social time doing things that they like. Often the most pleasant thing for us is to be near another human being in the same way that a cat socializes. When we talk about children doing this, we call it *parallel play*. Meaning hanging

out together but kinda doing our own thing. Be patient. Answer questions.

4) Transition into offering to teach life skills, gradually. Don't push it if they are not interested. I remember how incredibly confusing and complicated things like shaving, cooking, cleaning, and laundry felt at first. They are simple and easy now, but when I was younger I just couldn't understand why they were priorities or even important at all. It's hard for us to understand how cleanliness and appearance are measured and why. It doesn't mean we aren't interested or that we don't care. We just may have a longer learning curve and it takes a long time to relate the action to the reward. Think of it as helping someone write down all the unwritten rules.

5) Don't coddle. Trying to insulate an autistic person from the outside world is the number one thing that I've seen cause failure, across the board. In my experience, it seems that these efforts to keep someone "safe" and "happy" ultimately lead to them feeling helpless, rejected, dependent, and depressed.

6) Put them in intimate social situations with new people.

7) Laugh at their jokes.

8) Understand that their reactions to your behavior may not be empathic, and look past that. If their behavior feels awkward to you, it doesn't mean that they feel awkward. However, if you begin behaving awkwardly, they will internalize this against their self-esteem (e.g., "I am boring to hang out with"). It's also helpful to explicate what you are looking for. Say straight out, "I had a sad day and am feeling fragile, I don't need solutions

but I would love a little sympathy right now. Do you have the bandwidth for me to share?"

9) Don't push them in areas where they don't care. Instead, offer reasons why this might be important to them. For example, I didn't get my wisdom teeth taken out until I was 37 because no one could explain to me why I should do it. Encourage them to do their own research so it doesn't feel like you are enforcing your will. Not in a q-anon-rabbit-hole kind of way, but in a "your wisdom teeth are the most likely to grow in crooked and have perennial cavities, reducing the density of other teeth and causing problems with the jaw itself" kind of way. Having them investigate and make the ultimate decision for themselves is far more empowering than just insisting they do what the dentist says. It isn't that people resist change…we resist *being changed*. We all need to ultimately decide to change something because we're ready to and it makes sense to.

10) If they are interested, through CBT,[21] they can learn to intellectually mimic neurotypical communication methods. Anyone can learn what to look for and how to respond appropriately. In many ways learning to unpack other people's interpretations is like speaking to someone in *their* native language. It helps autistic people communicate better what we are feeling and experiencing as well.

11) Help them to find meaning and purpose and to invest deeply in it, so that they may eventually build a life around it

21 Faith wants to point out that while this process is referred to as CBT it really isn't CBT in the classic sense of the world. Therapists don't @ Joe for saying it is. We are well aware this is more skills training or SFBT or just classic BT in reality but insurance panels get their nipples hard for CBT and many people are trying to get their insurance to pay for their treatment so there we go.

and become an expert in it. Quirks and oddities will not matter anymore, if anyone even notices them. I had many very low points as an adult. I had experienced failure in all aspects of my life. I didn't care about anything because nothing meant anything, and I just wanted to die. But then I found my thing. Once you're deep enough in it, it doesn't matter what anyone else thinks, and self-consciousness becomes confidence.

12) If interested, find a support group for family members of autistic individuals. This way you can relate with people who genuinely understand, without imposing this on your family member.

My doctor strongly recommended ABA therapy—is that a good treatment for autism?

ABA was developed in the 1960s by psychologist Ole Ivar Lovaas. He was frustrated by the lack of care for autistic individuals and was trying traditional psychotherapy approaches with little success. Then he became a student of Sidney Bijou. Bijou was a classic behaviorist who was a student of B. F. Skinner. Yes, the Walden Two guy. Skinner was the guy who trained rats to push levers for pellets using a step-by-step process. And Bijou and Lovaas said, let's roll with that. (Or let's not. Because rats and autistic people are not the same. But we weren't there to argue with them, and they did roll with it.)

Lovaas' stated goal was to train austic children to "be normal." Instead, what he started doing was to train austic children, through really exhausting and confusing and sometimes downright cruel behavioral shaping methods, to mimic the behavior of non-neurodivergent people. But there was no context, no "why," behind the strategies.

Applied Behavior Analysis (ABA) is a method to use the brain's negative response to train out autistic behaviors, especially repetitive motions like stimming and outbursts from overwhelm. ABA is very effective at making parents feel more comfortable around their autistic children and creating the illusion that the child is integrating better into their environment. The reality is that it is doing this through traumatizing the child out of instinctive behaviors. Many adults report a positive experience from ABA, but keep in mind many people in abusive relationships report feeling a positive emotional relationship to their abusers. Imagine if you had screen time taken away or were shunned or yelled at each time that you did something that came naturally because it made other people uncomfortable.

The other problem is that this method doesn't work. In the long term, getting a ticket does not make someone less likely to speed. We don't even train dogs this way anymore, simply because the results are better when you focus solely on positive rewards for the desired behavior. ABA may appear to produce results, but at a price that isn't yet able to be determined.

If Joe had received ABA as a kiddo, Joe might have been trained to shake hands and make eye contact with an adult while being introduced, and say "Hi, I'm Joe Biel. Nice to meet you, what is your name?" Then the wanted behavior was rewarded and the autistic behaviors (like stimming) were punished.

But since the point of those interactions wasn't explicated, Joe might wander back off again before getting the answer. Or not know what to do with the answer. There wasn't any "When you know someone's name, you know which sound to make to get their attention . . . that's what names are for in their most basic form, like if I say 'hi Joe!' when you walk into a room, you know I am greeting you and not anyone else in the room or anyone coming in behind you," or "People like it when you remember their name, it demonstrates that you are paying attention to them and care about them and it is a good first step in making friends."

ABA is also incredibly intensive, up to 40 hours of work a week. Lovaas' research continued to show results, but only when autistic children got hours and hours and hours of ABA every week for long periods of time. Getting under 10 hours a week (which, *fuck*, is still a lot of time spent with an ABA therapist) did not achieve the same results.

Joe here again. Please, instead, listen to your child's emotional reactions. Understand what they are communicating. Encourage them to express their needs and understand what is going on inside of them to produce these reactions. This will require time and patience. Some autistic children become violent when overwhelmed. Put yourself in their shoes and think about how difficult their life is. Learn how to communicate in your own special way together. Understand their wants, needs, and reactions. Gradually, you can form a bond that meets each others' needs without fracturing or severing your relationship.

More from Faith: If you are feeling pressured to try ABA or you have run through other options and feeling pretty hopeless and want to give it a try, consider one of the newer versions of ABA therapy that are play-based instead of structured around oddly specific goals like "maintain eye contact for five full seconds" (which, uhhhh, no one does). Specifically look at the Early Start Denver Model and the Pivotal Response Training (PRT) model. Both are designed to work with a child's actual interests while building knowledge around social skills.

But please consider that there are many other ways to teach life skills without "behavioral shaping." All people, neurodivergent or not, are open to change. What we resist is *being changed*. If you are building your own means of communicating and listening, finding ways to teach skills within that framework will start to emerge. My youngest child, while not neurodivergent, definitely learns differently than traditional school methods allowed for. He would bring me whatever he was struggling with and ask "Could you explain this the way you explain things?" because he trusted me to understand and respect his confusion and help him process through it so he could learn and change in ways that made sense to him, not just to the adults around him.

How and why do allistics pathologize autistic people?

The first half dozen people that I (Joe) told about my diagnosis responded by telling me that the doctor was wrong. I internalized this gaslighting and stopped telling people for a long time. This diagnosis had been the greatest revelation of my life to date, and felt liberating in a way that I cannot simplify into words. Now, it's laughable to think that my "friends" would purport to know more about autism than a psychologist who specializes in it! This behavior remains a common problem because public awareness around autism is so minimal. Hearing, "Are you sure that you are autistic? You don't seem like you are autistic," is not quite daily anymore, but weekly. Worse, when people say these things it's because of ignorance and eugenicist thinking, based as much on not knowing what autism is as the presumption that being allistic is superior.

People who had known me for a long time and were a bit more reflective realized that the symptoms made sense and said things like, "Well, that really doesn't surprise me," and I became comfortable with telling people again. The results were mixed. Some were supportive and understanding, but as I became louder and more public, criticisms mounted. In what can only be summarized as ableism, many people began telling me that I was justifying every fuck up and odd behavior because of my "disease." One person, who saw me as a public figure, poignantly stated "Joe Biel is lame," in what she apparently meant as an ableist and derogatory remark, but if you ignore the slur, it is funny because it summarized the situation aptly. I respond to all of this by reverting back to facts and avoiding emotional arguments with people, educating the bystanders who are less hostile than someone who has their mind made up.

However, over time, this resulted in strangers dictating my experience. The thing about power is that the largest group dictates the terms. So, all autistic behavior and motives are interpreted through the lens of neurotypicals seeking to rationalize beliefs that are held, without allowing any conflicting information to influence their perspective. So if people cannot see you as autistic, they will defend and justify that belief through any explanation that suits this narrative.

And honestly? People's opinions of you are going to increasingly become none of your business. Meaning, you can't control the filter in which they view the world so if they made a decision about you that is counterfactual then fuck it.

Other people's concern happens because they cannot fathom how the symptoms might manifest in behaviors. Or in many telling examples, how all of our behaviors are literally triggers to indicate being suspicious to police officers, putting us at much heightened risks for being murdered.

Public attacks are painful, but the lack of awareness is apparent even in smaller, daily microaggressions. In public, strangers simultaneously assume that I am everything from nonverbal to intellectually disabled, while also being conniving, manipulative, and a predator because of everything from my posture to my gaze. I have been stopped on the street by strangers who have told me that it might be unsafe for me to be walking around unescorted. I would normally point to my service dog, partly as a joke. One woman told me that I could get robbed while walking from public transit to meet a friend. Once, in the airport, the woman behind me spoke very slowly in small words to try and convince me to let her hold my service dog while I went through security. If you're a neurotypical, my brain is different from yours, but let's not forget that I may also be smarter than you.

These kinds of encounters wear me down to a degree that I find myself choosing not to leave the house. It's exhausting.

What does it mean that autism causes rigidity? Is it common for autistic people to hate rules?

Autists learn primarily through a try/fail/try model of performing tasks. We try to do something in a way that seems logical or correct to us. It doesn't always work out how we intended and we refine our approach to attempt a better outcome next time. This process is painful and clunky and slow to evolve.

Autism isn't about loving/hating rules. It's like a managerial theory—autistic people interpret each request based on its supposed goals and how good the request is at achieving them. If we are working on a team with other people towards common goals, we need to understand what those goals are and why we are pursuing them. The goals can be big and bold and we can often operate within clearly stated parameters ("you'll never get into college if you stay home from school every day" or "please stamp this paperwork when it's been processed" or "never let the dog out").

Naturally, there are gray areas that arise for us in what might otherwise be a clear instruction or set of social norms for others. Working at a bookstore, we might be faced with three books with the same or very similar titles and we are supposed to assume the "logical choice" in figuring out which one the customer wants. That's beyond nebulous. How do I know? Consider autistic people as the ultimate constructivists, people who build their knowledge foundation from each new experience and piece of information.

Sometimes the thing that we are being asked to do will directly contradict existing rules that were initially outlined to us as firm. Sometimes the rules are pointless or directly contradict the goals that they supposedly serve. We are forward-focused and the way that we carry out tasks is rarely relational unless that corresponds to a set of rules. This is all to say that we rarely perform pointless tasks (without some significant training, conversation, or internal debate) solely for the purpose of making someone else happy.

We want to know why we are doing something and to know that our efforts will help with problems down the line. We don't want to gray up problems that are already less than black and white. Above all, we want consistency and logic. Give us clean rules that are consistent and we will follow them like no one you've ever known.

Sometimes we follow directions too literally, or the way that we interface with a problem hurts someone else's feelings. One of my favorite and most relatable examples of this is the woman who told her husband, "Don't let that man set foot on our property." The husband laid out boards so the man did not set foot on the property. He missed the nuance, which was that the wife didn't want the man to come over.

To most people, the husband would come across as a smartass, perhaps enacting some kind of willful punishment or revenge on his wife. But to an autist, this is following directions (albeit with rigidity).

I've worked with ASD employees who exhibit different kinds of rigidity. One has a complete meltdown if things are placed on or removed from her desk in her absence or if her supplies are pillaged by other staff. Another person requires you to put the date on any deadline. So for example, if you say, "Can I get these by Monday?" he will ask, "Can you please be more specific? Are you referring to Monday, April 22, 2097?"

Rigidity takes many forms. Mine has more to do with refusing to complete tasks or processes that perform a less-than-ideal function. I get so upset at bureaucracy and time-wasting that I often have a meltdown. I think of it as an ethical or political stance but in reality, it's that I cannot deal with systems that do not achieve their intended function. And while most people just see these tasks as "something that we all have to deal with," I cannot see past this. Rigidity is mostly commonly witnessed in routines. Some people cannot pick up the pen to start their work day until they have had coffee and cleaned their desk. It can be a major stressor to be interrupted by the mail arriving two minutes earlier than usual.

So, sure, everyone is rigid at times, but it often has more to do with having a personal boundary. For autists, the issue is much more deep-seated. Since we process 42% more information than neurotypicals, we have many more levels of code to review in our master decision-making programs.

This is due to the extreme volume of resting brain stimulus we receive. Some of us have better processing power and fewer maladaptions than others, which leads to greater levels of fluidity or frustration.

Generally speaking, someone who is autistic is not fucking with the person that they are asking for clarification from, they just genuinely don't want to answer or perform a task incorrectly (though, of course, if they think your question is silly, they just might be).

Is goal setting particularly hard for autistic adults?

Yes, connecting our meaning and purpose to individual goals and setting priorities for achieving them is often a disconnect for us, but over time this causation and correlation for happiness can be established and perfected.

Setting goals is easy but finding attachment or commitment to them can be a little more difficult. The most difficult part is that once you set a goal, the factors that made it desirable can change as other people move the goalposts. For example, 30 years ago I was skilled at setting up DIP switches for PC hardware, so people would hire me to set up their computer. In 1992, this felt like it would become my career but soon the implementation of plug-and-play computing turned this into a minimum wage job, because the computer learned to do the unnecessarily complicated things by itself. I was back to square one.

On one hand, it came too easily to me and I wasn't learning, so I tuned out. On the other hand, it was becoming a less-skilled job, so it was actually easier for an unskilled person to do. The jobs were gradually outsourced to India and China so no one wanted to pay me even $20,000 to do the work. It was a terrible early lesson in goal setting.

To this day, like many neurotypicals that I talk to, when a goal requires years of ongoing work, I do find myself doing other things instead of the most important or priority tasks. I clean my kitchen when I need to be writing, or organize my tools when I should respond to emails. These look like distractions, but (at least in my case) they help me to build up to and ease into the overwhelm of a major task that I am perhaps unfamiliar with all the moving parts of. Almost always, I find that even the most intimidating tasks are quite easy once I apply myself.

Fortunately, I found publishing, which is very complicated and contextual, and changes all the time. And it cannot be done by robots, though many have tried. I constantly have to be learning new things that both engage my brain and offer new ways to move complicated sets of finances and production values around. It's now a very easy goal to set and manage. I connected my meaning and purpose to my daily pursuits, as I care deeply about the subject matter of the work.

Once you find something you care about achieving, you must break down every goal into smaller and smaller individual tasks that you can sequence until you have things that you can do in five, ten, and sixty minutes until pursuing those goals is no longer challenging at all.

Faith jumping in here. There isn't a ton of research on goal setting and the specific needs of autistic individuals. One recent-ish study by Monica Carr and colleagues looked at how goal setting was taught as an applied skill to other neurodiverse individuals (e.g, ADHD) to find out if these same techniques could be of benefit for autistic folks. It's a well-considered study, noting that goal achievement for autistic individuals is not about intellect or academic capability, but is more a function of behavior, time, and task management while in pursuit of a goal. If the question becomes "is goal setting a learnable skill for autistic folks?" the short answer is yes.

And goal-setting is a valuable component of self-determination. Self-determination is important because it allows you to "function independently" in a way that is meeting the requirements and comfort level of those around you. It means you are in control of your own life.

Many of the coaching tools that help an autistic person understand goal setting include:

- An independent will to achieve a particular goal. Meaning it is the autistic person's goal, not someone's goal for them

- Identifying what makes a goal attainable

- Goal contracting (making a commitment to the process)

- Understanding the relationship of time to goal achievement

- Self-management strategies

- Self-monitoring and progress tracking
- Reinforcement and support and feedback from the coach

The goal setting tool we have in Dr. Faith's workbook zine *Achieve Your Goals* is structured and creates space for many of these needs. The coaching support could be a friend, family member, therapist, life coach, accountability buddy—anyone who is willing and able to help the autistic individual strengthen this particular skill set.

Why are so many autistic people sexual and gender minorities?

Joe here. I'm autistic and not cisgender. I don't use pronouns to talk about myself and tried, for a time, to convince others to do this too. It became more exhausting to correct people than to let it pass. Fundamentally, I want people to respect me and where I'm coming from, not recite facts back to me. Correcting people incessantly only further isolates me, causes me to lose ground and respect, and takes us away from any point that I was trying to make. Of course, correcting others incessantly may be correct and necessary for you to establish your identity and self-respect.

Gender identity becomes so wrapped up in autistic identity that the term "autigender" was created to identify this growing group of autists. The strange thing is that, perhaps since we are an emerging group during a series of culture wars, many trans people will tell us that we aren't "really" trans, that this is just us being weird, or an "autistic preoccupation," or trying to glomb onto another emergent trend. Queer people are protective of their communities because they have been under attack for centuries. Still, it can be rather exhausting to carve out your own space and have to defend it from other marginalized people who are afraid that you are trying to claim a piece of their pie. At the same time, 90% of autistic people that I've met under 30 are not cisgender. Only 30% of autistic people that I know under 40 are cis. The numbers continue in this trajectory as they get older, and this seems to be about self-awareness and the generational cultural freedom to express yourself that wasn't yet available to older generations. You know. Boomers.

Anecdotal evidence aside, let's have Faith walk us through how many ASD individuals are sexual or gender minorities. So, first of all, we don't know how big the overlap is. The studies indicate that it's somewhere between 4 and 26%, which is a big spread. Studies differentiate in rigor, and many are using only a screening tool versus a full assessment to "diagnose" the aforementioned autism. And in other studies there is only one question about gender at all (the Child Behavior Checklist has a question for parents asking if the child has expressed a desire to "be of the opposite sex.")

That being said, Faith has two questions for you:

1) Do *you* think it's a thing? Meaning, do you think they are related, and your autism has shifted your gender identity formation?

2) If so . . . does it matter?

I ask these questions right off the bat, because while there is a significant overlap between being neurodivergent and falling somewhere under the trans umbrella, correlation is not causality. Meaning they co-exist but that doesn't mean that one thing caused the other. In truth, we don't know. Researchers since the 1990s have been studying the link and posited theories, like one that struggles with social interaction cause "atypical" gender identity formation.

Which (1) Why are we labeling recognizing oneself as not being cis considered "atypical?" Atypical means *not representative of the norm.* And throughout human history, there have always been people who understood their own gender outside an immutable binary. Like autism itself, that word pathologizes a common human experience. Being less prevalent shouldn't equate to atypicality in either neurodiversity or gender identity.

And (2) to presume causality and etiology of gender incongruence is a huge and weird cognitive leap to make, based solely on the fact that gender identity formation remains flexible in younger kids. Younger kids (neurodivergent or not) are always exploring their place and role in the world, and sometimes younger kids who express uncertainty do shift back and settle into a cis identity by puberty. Again? This is normal. When we don't fit in, for any reason, we question why. I have not seen any studies that show that the same people who are demonstrating X level of struggles with social interaction have Y levels of gender incongruence. It's really a "fuck if we know, here's our best guess" theory. That originated decades ago, before we knew as much as we know now about autism and transgender identities.

The argument that gender incongruence is really just autistic perseveration is just as philosophical as *my* argument. Which is that if you are on the autism spectrum, you have already realized you're different. You don't read people well. They're weird and complex and you become less and less interested in social norms. So why not lean into your authenticity and express your true gender, if you already know you don't really fit in anyway?

I have worked with many people who were assigned a gender at birth and continue to wear it as a costume day-in and day-out because that's the expectation. It's just easier for them to not transition, at least at this point in their lives. It's both heartbreaking and totally understandable. But of my non-cis clients who are also neurodivergent? That's never been a consideration. I've heard over and over variations on the theme of "I've never fit in, so why try to conform to anything? Why not just be me?" My opinion is that the causality debate is just a tributary of the current raging river of society's trans identity moral panic. And the reality is not nearly the issue people think it is.

Which brings us back to our original questions. If you are worried that you are conflating these identities in yourself, it might be helpful to work with a therapist who specializes in gender so you can safely do some discernment work without judgment. But I also offer you the second question. It's based on a conversation my husband and I had about ten years ago about the "gender as autistic perseverance" kerfluffle. What he said was *"Who the fuck cares? If transitioning helps someone, let them transition, dammit!"*

Reader? *You* can totally see why I married him, right? The world is already really, really hard. Let's not create more problems. We need to listen to people's lived experience and respect their domain of their bodies. We don't need so many checkpoints for care. Non-surgical interventions for gender affirming care are based on informed consent. Do the informed part and advocate for what you need. If you are a family member reading this and you are worried about your loved one? Talk to them about it. But then do the informed part and advocate for what they need.

Where and how can autistic folks who've been super sheltered learn basic life skills like finances, hygiene, housekeeping, cooking, or timeliness?

The same way that any other person would: Based on your learning style and tolerance for other people. Meaning, that being autistic doesn't change the fact that everyone learns differently. Some people learn best by hearing, others by seeing, yet others by doing. I (Faith) am a hands-on, tactile learner. Reading the directions or watching a YouTube video only gets me so far. Eventually I have to jump in and make a big mess and figure things out, unfortunately. This isn't a huge deal if I am putting together a bookshelf. If chemicals are involved, a human who does know what they are doing needs to be assigned to me for my own protection.

In community mental health, these in-person learning methods are called "skills training" if you are under eighteen and "psychosocial rehabilitation" if you are over eighteen. I don't know who came up with those terms, but the idea is that a trained case manager can help you learn any life skills you are struggling with so you can lead a life of more independence. I was a case manager for many years before going to grad school, so I can tell you it's a broad umbrella and you don't have to feel bad for needing help with skills no one ever taught you. *Everyone* is having to learn these skills in some way, shape, or form.

One of my favorite stories is about my skills client being so frustrated and overwhelmed with her new job at Sonic and her worry that she wasn't going to remember all the recipes for the drink combos. I had picked her up from work and she was tearful that she was going to get fired and she was so proud to be working. We sat down and made a chart of all the drink combo ingredients for her to keep at her work station. She was worried everyone would tease her about her "cheat sheet," but instead everyone thought it was super cool and useful and wanted copies of it for themselves . . . her boss praised her organization and innovation!

So if you are thinking, "That's nice but I don't think Faith is going to fly out and organize my life for me, where do I start?," let's go back to our original question about how you learn. If you start by reading, good websites to start learning something are: Instructables, eHow, wikihow, r/howto, HomeTips, and Quora. If you do better at watching videos, YouTube is still the biggest but there are also Vimeo and TikTok.

You also may be able to take a class or get a coach. Life skills for adults are typically provided through community health clinics in the U.S. If the skills are specific to gaining and maintaining employment, you may be able to access them through whomever provides the county's supported employment in your area. There may be other agencies doing amazing work, especially if you are in a metropolitan area. If you are looking for your own psychosocial rehab case manager to help you in person, getting that covered by insurance will require that damn diagnosis thing again (see that section if you skipped it the first time around).

Finding these resources may feel very daunting and overwhelming and that's because it is. In the U.S., call the 211 helpline (a free public health and human services referral number). Now, let's get you ready to call, OK?

1) First off, get a pen and paper and make sure the pen works. If you type faster than you write and you can put your phone on speaker or you have earbuds so you can talk and type that's fine, too. Just be ready to talk and type or talk and write.

2) Call 211. If they say their name when they answer, write it down. If they answer "211 Blah Blah service, how may I help you" ask them (politely) "Thank you! To whom am I speaking?" And write it down.

3) Once you have their name, say "Thank you, [their name]! This is [your name]. I'm an adult and I am autistic and I am looking for a program that can help teach me life skills. I live in [county you live in]. Can you help me find programs that I might qualify for?"

4) They will read off information. It's OK to ask them to slow down as you write. Also, take your time to repeat the information back to them. Then thank them again, by name.

5) If you want to build good relationships in a frustrating system? Ask them to transfer you to their supervisor's voicemail so you can leave a message telling their supervisor that they were helpful and professional. No, you don't have to do this. But they will adore you and remember you forever and help you with whatever you need whenever you call back and they answer the call. This is a trick that Faith used as a case manager for over a decade and could always get whatever she needed for her clients through her relationships in the community. And basically, you're learning to be your own case manager, here. If you want to do this you would say "I was really worried that this would be a difficult process, but you were so helpful and considerate, and I really appreciate it! Would you transfer me to your direct supervisor so I can let them know how much you helped me and how patient you were with me today, [name]? I know supervisors generally only hear complaints and rarely the good stuff."

6) Now you have a list of programs and may want to research them online if you are comfortable with that. It's also entirely OK to ask a trusted friend or family member to help you sort through them all, if that helps you manage data overwhelm. Some people process really well that way, some people feel very

overwhelmed sorting through websites. At least they don't all have flashing graphics and awful midi-music anymore.[22] If it makes your brain feel like you're looking at gibberish, you can start calling programs directly, totally fine. Just like calling 211, you're going to keep an even bigger list of information so keep your pen or laptop handy, still, OK?

7) Same thing as before, when you call, listen for their name and write it down or if they don't say it ask for it and write it down and greet them by name while offering yours. Such as "Hi, [their name]! This is [your name!]! I was referred to you by [name of person] from the 211 service! I am looking for a skills training program for autistic adults. It's for me, I am self-referring, and I would like to get some more information on what I need to do to qualify for services, what the program costs, and what insurance plans you accept. Can you or someone else there help me with that?"

8) Most places will be really good about giving you the scope of the program, but not always. You may have some specific questions that they aren't used to answering like "I don't drive, but I'm comfortable taking the bus, how close are you to a bus line?" or "I work at the animal shelter during the day, do you have any evening or weekend classes?"

---

22 If you are young enough to not remember this, Buddha bless. The early days of html coding were pretty . . . exhausting for people who just wanted to find contact info.

9) It's entirely OK to be politely persistent. If you are moving down the list, and you find that you are being referred to in a circle (meaning one place referred you to another place which referred you back to the first place) just say that. This is where having names comes in handy. As in "Oh yes! [Name] at [Place One] had told me to contact you, I spoke with her earlier, so if you are full too, can you think of any other options?" If they don't, you can ask if they have a waiting list or ask if there is a time that you can call back for a slot (then make sure you put it on your calendar so you remember to call back).

10) You can also do the transfer-me-to-your-supervisor-so-I-can-compliment-your-help thing here. Again, it will go hugely far in getting you information, support, or a spot in a program you really want to get into in exchange for a 30 second message. Most people who do this work are terribly underpaid and get fussed all day long and will remember you and think really lovely things about you for this kindness (though obviously don't do this if they are shitty and rude).

This is a lot and I'm sorry it's so difficult to get something you need to be successful in life. We'd rather you fight to get it than struggle without it. Don't give up if this is something that will make a huge difference in your independence, success, and happiness.

How can an autistic person get by independently if they have neuroception issues that make it dangerous to do some basic life skills, like cooking?

Faith's husband is not neurodiverse. He is, however, very very klutzy on stairs, as discovered when we moved into a new house this summer. After making sure nothing was sitting on the stairs, changing the lighting on the stairs, and checking his blood sugar we finally just admitted to ourselves that his depth perception is kinda trash and I bought him some grippy socks. And I am putting a decal on the last stair that says "last stair." I guess the other option would be to put up a husband-sized baby gate and make him live downstairs. But that seems a bit extreme of a solution for a grown-ass person who just needs a little scaffolding and problem-solving, doesn't it?

And we all need scaffolding. I need reading glasses, an alarm clock, and a step stool for certain parts of my home. And me saying this only elicits a "well, sure" response, right? Everyone needs some support for basic life skills for whatever reason. Why would that be different for an autistic person?

Neuroception means the way your brain decides, faster than you can think consciously, if someone or something is dangerous or safe. If you don't neurocept well because of autism, that means you have to learn those skills concrete-as-pavement. And you absolutely can. And we can add scaffolding for support as needed. It's entirely OK to use pre-prepped ingredients. Or an entire meal kit. Or use the crockpot instead of the stove and oven. Or maybe a learned rule to look for the light indicator on the stove that a burner is still hot.

Whatever grippy socks and "last stair" decals you need to gain or maintain some independence is just as fine for you (or your loved one) as it is for my klutzy husband and my short, blurry-eyed, overly-tired self. Competent skills training (see question above) involves personalizing the experience to the human being who is receiving it, no matter the original cause.

(And yes, the socks worked perfectly . . . he hasn't fallen again.)

Can autistic people enjoy poetry? Do autistic people like to have fun?

The law is fairly forgiving in this regard. Autistic people are allowed to enjoy whatever we want that is legal in our jurisdiction, though the NT disability bias would almost always tell you otherwise.

Everyone likes to have fun. It's just that the world built a wall between us and our fun. And we are trying to scale that impasse in every which way, which makes no sense to neurotypicals. That's fine. We learn to accept this with time.

Of course, it goes without saying that what I do for fun isn't what you do for fun, and what you do for fun isn't what your grandpa did for fun. We have different brains. We interact with data differently. We socialize differently, and social skills can be like eggshells for us that are triggering and painful.

As a child in the 80s, I (Joe) was very excited about the invention of Atari and spent a lot of time with my imagination, following blocks around a maze, imagining that they were dragons, swords, and treasures. Later, I learned to play the drums, which put me in the awkward situation of socializing with my band members. They decided that I should sing instead, which I did, but then I had to learn how to move and perform like a frontperson. I finally did, just as the band broke up. But first, one childhood friend put it "I thought you were playing the stereo really loud and then I looked and your band had gotten good!" It was fun for minutes at a time as a teenager, but was mostly full of heartache and pain. Now I mostly enjoy spreadsheets, book publishing, drinking tea, reading, talking in small groups, and writing on Quora.

Who doesn't like to have fun?

Why do autistic people not usually follow fashion norms?

From a very young age I dressed practically, often in clashing colors and styles. I once famously wore red sweat pants and a clashing red shirt to school for Valentine's Day after being told to "wear red." I remember thinking that I was really killing it. Everyone else wore very minimal amounts of red or pink as a small aspect of detail in their outfit. I was mortified and even made fun of by my teachers.

I wore boots instead of more fashionable footwear due to my walk to school. As I grew up, I was excited when grunge and punk came into fashion as those sloppy looks were much easier for me to navigate as a teenager. I could shop at thrift stores and clashing and ugly clothes *were* finally killing it! I always preferred pleated pants for comfort and fit as I was very tall and very skinny and fashionable jeans were painfully tight and looked terrible on me.

Now I'm very particular about my fibers. I cannot wear a t-shirt with a low thread count because it feels like sandpaper. I prefer poly-blends and have much more pressing concerns than fashion norms. But I've branched out and now think of myself as trendsetting and fashion forward. I wore fluorescent fanny packs from about 1985–2015, watching them become cool again, during the middle of that period!

I now gravitate towards wearing a few different bright colors for my own enjoyment. I wear tailored clothes, mostly for comfort and because I finally have the budget for it. Creating my own style increased my own confidence, which really helps me in public with my self-esteem.

Just like rules that don't make sense, I see most fashion as nonsensical and most of the fashion norms as ugly and impractical. For the past 30 years I have cut my hair daily to create wild and elaborate hairstyles with a lot of body. As I age out of a reasonable range to wear fluorescent clothes, fanny packs, t-shirts, and fitted pants, I am frequently mistaken for someone twenty years younger.

No one sets fashion trends by following fashion norms. Fashion is established by someone setting sail with a bold new look that will be hated just as much as it is loved and embraced. Autistics are classic inventors so it makes perfect sense that we are fashion forward and focused on the details that others miss.

Best of all, my fashion is constantly complimented by people older and younger than myself. I cannot always tell if/when they are joking. But I don't care.

Faith jumping in here. My oldest child had sensory issues with their clothes before they could walk and talk. They still do. As a toddler, we went with whatever they could tolerate on their skin that day if we were going out, and if we were inside I just let them be naked. They need clothes to be soft and comfortable. Flannel is a big favorite. They were in a deep panic a few years back after taking a job that required them to wear all black. I suggested two options: Asking for an ADA accommodation letter from their therapist or buying some black dye and dying a few of their flannels black. We chose the latter and they were able to be comfortable and follow the in-house dress code.

So what we're both saying here is . . . there are reasons your brain and body may not be comfortable in the hip new thing;. And fuck it, be comfortable. Comfortable is good for confidence and you will get much further than if you are uncomfortably fashion-forward. Everyone can always tell when you don't feel good in your own skin.

What is the best thing that being autistic has taught you?

The tendency to always question everything. It's something that I (Joe) bring to every situation that I encounter in life, and has mostly resulted in my being constantly shouted down for being difficult, nonconforming, and obstinate. It drove me out of schools, social activities, relationships, and a marriage.

Now that I'm middle-aged and managing a business, this best practice of always asking "Why?" has diverted me away from danger more times than I can count. Microcosm is growing over 100% year over year these past three years, in a publishing industry trying to manage losses and where almost all of our peer businesses fail. Questioning why each decision makes sense, or more specifically, asking "what is the goal and what is the easiest way to get there?" has eliminated so much busy work and so many tasks that simply never bear fruit or haven't ended up functioning as intended.

Strangest of all, whenever I explain this basic business and life hack to people and explain how it removes barriers to success, they eternally respond, "It must be nice," or "How lucky that worked out," or most often "But I don't want to." Even when we reveal our poker hand and explain exactly how to recreate our successes, people's emotions prevent them from seeing that our decisions are borne of data, experience, and trial-and-error. Emotional decision making prevents their success.

I don't have it all figured out, but our average book sells double the industry average (despite having much smaller budgets). We can reveal all of our statistics and data with no risk of our ideas being repeated or implemented elsewhere in a way that harms us. So it allows us to share freely!

My autistic daughter really wants to work in a zoo or animal sanctuary. Will any of those places hire her?

Of course! The biggest part of the issue is for your daughter to understand that she's part of the 1.5% and that certain things are easier for her and other things are more difficult for her than for other people.

For example, I (Joe) cannot hold a job for very long because I cannot make myself follow rules that don't serve their stated goal. But I set up my own organization where I could set my own cultural priorities. I struggle with personal relationships and communication, but I read books and learned how to manage people. I now have a partner who is more suited for this task and enjoys it while I pursue things I excel at. But it was important to see that I could do it.

Your daughter may be as unhappy and unsuited for a managerial job as I was. But she might find true joy in helping the animals through an administrative role where her focus on details could make her excel. Or, she may enjoy a deeper personal relationship with the animals directly, through their care and feeding. This is something that autistic people are often suited for, as animals' emotional expression and needs are often easier for us to read than people's.

There are many employers and institutions that are unfriendly and even hostile towards autistic employees. While the ADA protects your daughter, it's not necessarily worthwhile to get involved in a fight for one's rights with someone that is going to treat you poorly anyway. There are employers out there who can recognize what your daughter can offer. Or she may end up making her own way, like I did. Like setting up her own pet sitting/walking service or her own doggie daycare where she can care for the animals she loves with the time and attention they deserve. In the meantime, she might begin by offering this service to neighbors, where she sets the terms of the arrangements and learns social skills.

WHAT'S THE DEAL WITH SOCIAL SKILLS?

How can neurotypicals do a better job of getting along with autistic people?

Joe here. The biggest problem is that neurotypicals try to relate with autistic people in the same way that they relate with other NTs. When we don't respond in the expected manner, they begin to assume we don't understand or have deep-seated psychopathic tendencies. They want to have a conversation where we are forced to learn their foreign language. Of course we don't understand what they're talking about or respond in the way that they expect. For us, words literally have different meanings and they hold all of the privileges. For example, "How are you doing today?" is the most sociopathic and misleading question that the NT industrial complex ever conspired to ask. To them it appears to mean merely "Hello." To us it's a spring-loaded bear trap set on extracting our deepest fears and emotions. And when we dare to follow directions and unload our vulnerabilities on them, they stare at us like *we* are the asshole. We exist with both a different language and culture. This is why we find NTs so confusing and unpleasant.

Before we become intellectually aware of the emotional minefield of NT communication habits, emotional gripes sound like a problem posed to us to solve. "My friend really hurt my feelings" may beget a "Perhaps you shouldn't be friends anymore." Which is so emotionally loaded to an NT and is more likely to make a painful situation worse that after a few encounters like this with an autistic person, NTs often judge us as being insensitive, cruel, or manipulative.

We need clearer phrasing, not clouded by nonverbal communication, figures of speech, or emotional weight and expectations. We need patience and the other person to get in our head. Our communication and interpretation styles defy their intuition about the nature of relationships. More often than n0t, the emotional expression of autistic people is misunderstood by NTs. We appear sad or angry when we are not. We appear stoic when we are stewing or deeply upset. When we think something is funny, they think we are complaining. In general, neuroception (the pre-conscious ability to predict someone else's intentions) isn't serving NTs either, since they often read each other wrong too. I wonder how many neurotypical relationships have been destroyed by a misinterpretation of someone else's emotional state or intentions where nobody bothered to talk it out afterwards. NTs are disabled like that.

How can autistic people set boundaries to protect ourselves?

Joe again with some bad news. Trust me, this next one is a doozy that makes no sense. But believe me. NTs are really hung up on how they *feel* over the actual *reality of what happened*. Yes, you read that correctly. Their emotions build the bridge of their experience. They have an emotional reaction to stimuli before they have an intellectual one. This is how a neurotypical brain works. It's meant to make sure that emotions operate as a warning system for danger and a marker for things that make them happy.

The problem with this is that NTs don't care what the motive or intent of your action or statement was. They care what the impact of your words or actions were. Yes, I'm aware that makes no sense. No, arguing about this with them will not end anywhere good. Trust me. I've tried. They are really weird.

Part of the reason that arguing with others about what's for them is ineffective is that you simply don't have information to know those things. However, you do know what's best for yourself. You have a right to make mistakes and do things that other people don't agree with. This is your locus of control. You cannot control the world around you or change other people's actions but you can choose your words and actions to approach what's right for yourself in each situation. This is a major stumbling block that I run into with autistic teens and twenty-somethings that I mentor. They want to create a system of order for the world that just doesn't exist. For example, "I followed the rules. Now I want this other person to do what I want . . . or at least follow the rules. Can you make them do that?" But that's not how it works. We cannot control other people no matter how much easier it would make our lives or how upsetting their behavior is. I agree that other people should respect you but, instead, when they do not, you have to implement boundaries to protect yourself and give them a reason to respect you. If someone else is rude to you, distance yourself from them, even if you thought that you'd be friends. If someone is harassing you, stand up for yourself by saying something like "Why are you being a dick?"

Ultimately, we can't control other people, only ourselves and how we interact with them. Take a look at this handy reference of things that you can and cannot affect and plan your life accordingly:

THINGS I CANNOT CONTROL

• other people's choices

• other people's words

• other people's reactions to my words and choices

• who wants to be my friend

THINGS I CAN CONTROL

people who I try to befriend • how I react to my feelings • what I put in my body • my choices • how I express myself • who I keep in my life • who I am intimate with • how I spend my time

• who agrees to have sex with me

• other people's feelings

• other people's ideas

When you start to create boundaries and a locus of control, you'll get carried away at first, saying "no" simply because you can. Start by adjusting it to "No, thank you." Then, with time, try to learn to moderate that and think about what you need and what you want and realize the power of this choice to reduce your own anxiety and meltdowns. You probably know what places are stressful or painful for you. You can probably avoid them more often than not. You probably know where you like to go and what you like to eat and who makes you feel good. You can choose to spend more time around those things and people even if others don't think these are good choices for you. You have a right to make mistakes. Making your own choices, even if some of them are mistakes, is the most important part of being an adult.

Sometimes a line like "If you say/do that one more time, I'm going to walk away/disengage from this relationship, etc" has a surprising amount of power. The trouble is that you have to consider the costs and consequences up front, be comfortable with all outcomes, and uphold your end of the bargain based on the other person's choices.

I have trouble relating to others and socializing because of my autism. Can I change this?

In our first social skills CBT session my (Joe's) psychiatrist handed me a piece of paper titled "rules for successful socializing." It outlined some very helpful rules that applied to all situations. Here are my paraphrases:

- Ask questions about the other person whenever your instinct is to talk about your interests.

- Consider what others are saying more than thinking about your own responses.

- Try to relate your own knowledge and experiences only after they have stopped talking for a full second.

- Closely evaluate the body language and facial expressions of the other person when you are talking.

- Don't share too much too soon, especially if you have very intense recent events in your personal life.

- Pay attention to how much other people are talking and contribute, but speak less frequently than others.

- Don't share too much too soon, especially if you have very intense recent events in your personal life.

- Think about the why someone brings something up or changes the subject, especially if it seems abrupt or steeped in metaphor. They may be expressing discomfort with the previous subject or speaking in neurotypical secret code.

- Unless you know someone very well, avoid contentious topics that may end the conversation.

- If the conversation moves away from your interests, listen and offer nonverbal communications instead of changing the subject.

- Never talk for more than two sentences unless you are telling a story or someone has specifically asked you to answer a question about an area of your own expertise.

I still live by this last rule first and foremost. It keeps me focused in my thoughts, and helps me edit down my rhetorical rants to just the simplified version of what I want to say. And it helps me socialize better with anyone, especially neurotypicals. Except Faith, who finds rhetorical rants amusing.

It takes a little practice at first. But gradually it taught me the value of listening. Most people are not very good at prioritizing their hierarchy of information and don't see communication as a way of exchanging relevant information. They are trying to relate emotionally to each other, which isn't really of interest to people like us. But we can learn to roll with it. Practice will train you how to do this better.

The most magic phrase I've learned is, "I feel [some kind of way] when you [insert their behavior]." Talk about how other people's behavior affects you and be receptive to hearing the same in return. Internalize feedback they give you and learn from it. Change your approach around it in the future. When you are alone, put your thoughts and feelings together. This will allow you to really figure out how you would like others to treat you, and how the way you treat people makes them feel, based on the feedback that you've received.

Be prepared. Because you will be treated to their feelings in return. But these conversations are often very positive and illuminating. It allows you to become closer, lets them know about you, and extends the offer for them to share things with you.

When you are in a group setting, divide the amount of time that you will spend together by the total number of people present. This is the *maximum* amount of time that you are allowed to talk. Speaking less is ideal, but you still want to engage the conversation and speak some. Not speaking enough and speaking too much both result in people not relating to you or thinking that you are playing a strange game of withholding. Other people will not follow these rules but this isn't the point. You are improving your social habits to better engage with other people so they can relate with you.

I've found that telling stories to NTs helps them to better relate with us, and to better understand the people they love who are on the spectrum. This is why I wrote my book, *Good Trouble*, which details how to overcome the social disabilities of autism, how to create healthy relationships after adult diagnosis, as well as the many ways that the symptoms have created pain and failure in my life. It's the same reason I give frequent interviews on the topic; so that other autistic people feel less alone, and so that NTs can better understand our lived experience and stop pathologizing us. By creating a trail of breadcrumbs, we can help others fit in better in a neurotypical world.

Can autistic people feel empathy?

Absolutely. It's just accessed differently. Others' feelings can often be harder to relate to our own experiences at first. For this reason, our empathy is often best accessed intellectually. This is done by understanding what an appropriate response is, as well as understanding the disconnect between our motives and our impact.

This is why we are often mistaken as having no empathy, like a sociopath. We are rigid and can become argumentative easily. This can hurt other people who are already upset and can make it seem like we don't care. We do care, but our own emotions can combine with other stimuli to overwhelm us and shut us down. It's difficult to unpack the nuance of what is being expressed, especially if it's being said nonverbally.

We also categorically face severe anxiety and depression which further compound the desperation present in every social interaction that we have. Remember how simple social "questions" like "How are you doing?" are incredibly complex because they absolutely are misleading and don't mean what they purport to.

"How are you?" (and its unhelpful variations) are the most complicated questions for several reasons. It's impossible to know what information is being sought because the question is so broadly interpretable. Most people who ask don't want to know, or at least want a one-word answer that alleviates their social responsibilities. I understand that you want more than that, but it's still inherently complicated. On the base layer, I have to single handedly determine:

- How much depth is sought and is there time for?

- What I am giving and what I am receiving?

- How much backstory is necessary?

- How good is this person's memory to understand the context and history of these events?

- Will they understand certain life experiences or will I have to unpack how things are different for me than for them?

- How much is this person is going to argue about basic aspects of my experience?

It's a question where I am almost always accused of intentionally not providing the response that the person wanted, when they take no responsibility for not asking the specific question for the information that they actually wanted. It's a situation where I can only lose.

The strangest aspect of "How are you?" is that if you actually answer the question, neurotypicals tend to interpret you unloading these details *at their specific request* to communicate that you don't have capacity to talk about how *they* are doing. This often frustrates them or makes them feel like you are emotionally unavailable, regardless of the truth. All of these factors create a very painful cycle, especially when we are accused of having no empathy as a result.

What are uncommon early intervention strategies to help autistic children be more sociable? My daughter who is six screams until she gets her way.

The problem is two-fold: Your daughter is likely expressing her emotions, not trying to influence yours. You don't want to discourage her from expressing herself, but you also don't want to reward screaming until she gets the Oompa Loompa she is demanding. So your job here is to simultaneously encourage her to continue communicating emotions and needs, without rewarding screaming. Slowly shape these requests until she has a less reactive way of getting what she needs.

Throughout childhood, caretakers, parents, teachers, authority figures, and counselors tend to respond to autistics in one of two ways: sheltering and coddling or abusing us. These experiences imprint upon our brains and influence how we form behavior and best practices, like they do for any child. Parents are often bewildered when left with a childish, dependent adult who lacks confidence and cannot take care of themselves, or a resentful adult with a series of maladaptive ways of attempting to get our needs met. Nobody wants this, and it's not serving anybody, so a middle ground must be found if we are to become independent, confident adults.

In a sick way, I (Joe) realized that being abused as a child is what taught me this kind of agency. While I do not recommend this way of learning, the constant bullying and abuse eventually taught me to say "no" and to stand up and advocate for myself. I ran away and slowly figured out how to take care of myself on my own, finding people that cared about me as well as morals and a value system in punk rock. I had no other choice of how to stay alive in the world. I was lucky that I did.

Last week, I was approached by two different parents of autistic children. One father had just found out that one of his five children was autistic. He is a single father and not a typically sensitive case. He had played football and now played poker for money. He was a man's man, so I was a little hesitant to offer advice because I wasn't sure that it would be heard.

I offered him some resources and he listened closely and was responsive. It became clear that despite all of his other responsibilities, he was deeply committed to the experience of his autistic son being a good one, at almost any cost to himself.

The other father who got in touch had a different problem. He was concerned about how his other children were reacting to the different treatment that he gave his autistic son and worried that the other children might not be as understanding as they had a wide variety of interests and experiences. He wanted advice on how to talk to them, again because he was invested in the experience of his autistic son that he largely could not empathically relate to but still wanted his son to have a strong upbringing.

Now I bring up these two examples because most of the stories told to me about the parents of autists are terrible. They involve being ignored, trapped, mistreated, coddled, isolated, or pushed out. And naturally, these are the kind of stories that we are going to be told. No one is going to find it notable to tell the story of the good parent who is attentive to creating a positive upbringing for their autistic child. Naturally though, they are out there. Thank you for being one of them.

As for your daughter, I'd suggest validating her emotions and comforting her. E.g., "I can see that you're really upset. This must be really painful for you. Do you want to talk about why this is so upsetting?" If it's in public and you need to leave where you are . . . leave where you are. You must also not allow yourself to be manipulated, as it seems likely that this is what she learned from your previous rewarding of her behaviors.

For example, when I was a kid, I expected to receive a coloring book whenever I went to the grocery store. Maybe this had been promised and delivered once or twice and I came to expect it. If I didn't get one, I would scream until I did. I could not understand, however, that some grocery stores simply didn't have coloring books. What kind of global conspiracy was this?

When your daughter is not upset, pursue the conversation again. "Can you talk about why that was so upsetting?" Often, for us, it's upsetting when schedules change unexpectedly or what we think to be true turns out not to be. Inconsistencies feel unfair. It's legitimately difficult to turn on a dime. We like routines and reliability and we rely on expectations. That might be part of the issue, but engaging this as a conversation and listening to her should be able to prevent these upsetting situations from arising in the first place.

Your daughter will likely cherish the ability to have a say in her own life and to prevent upsetting circumstances from coming up. By rewarding positive behavior, you'll both be happier.

Take a lesson from Geel, the town in Belgium where mental health was not stigmatized but treated as part of some people's life cycle: accept your child the way she is. There's a great story from Geel of a man who imagines that he's being pursued by a bull, and his friend, instead of telling him it's not real, fights off the imaginary bull. Rather than feeling gaslit and stigmatized, he feels safe and comforted. It's much more powerful to give positive encouragement where appropriate than to push or try to impose your own reality.

Fight off every bull threatening your child, make them feel loved, take away the pressure from emotional investment. Allow kids to develop at their own pace, support their strengths, and give encouragement without being forceful. Most important, allow your child to see that they can trust you to meet their needs.

In these situations, make your child feel heard by listening to them and taking their answers at face value rather than as metaphorical or blame-dodging. Things that an autistic child will say may not make sense to you or may seem like a diversion. But that is their experience, stress, and even trauma.

For example, when I have spent more than ten hours over a 48 hour period in the presence of other people or outside of my expected routines, it's a subtle escalation of my stress all day long and I'm highly reactive, even to things that wouldn't have bothered me otherwise. I am left with the choice to bottle up my feelings or snap at people, both of which have severely negative consequences. Instead, I need to plan ahead to prevent this. I'm attentive enough to notice it now in middle age, but as a child who wasn't allowed to make choices about my time, it was an incredible stressor. I wasn't aware that I *had* emotions, let alone that other people did, so it became very difficult to rationally explain why I was so upset to my parents, who would routinely dismiss them anyway.

I would get punished for my childhood meltdowns, which only worsened and escalated them. Gradually, it led me to feel like literally no one understood me, and that I would be punished for who I was fundamentally; things that I could not help or change. This was repeated in adult relationships, creating further pathologizing.

Now I can understand my parents' frustration and confusion, but at the time it felt very me against them. So listen to your child and take them at face value. Adapt your approach. Talk to your other children, and teach them why it's vital for them to accommodate this worldview. And once they fully understand the issue, if your autistic child is still being an asshole, level with them: "Listen, I know that you're having a crappy day but we agreed on some solutions and we both need to honor them." If you are both doing the best you can, progress will happen. Just don't put the entire burden of their condition on them.

Is it okay to tell people that I am autistic?

This is a common fear so let's look at it a different way: most people you tell this to will already have some sense that you are different and it will not be a surprise to them. You will rarely shock someone and admittedly the most difficult responses are from the people who do not see you as disabled and thus try to be empathetic and relational by telling you that "you don't *seem* autistic." In most cases, this is a product of them not understanding what autism is and how it looks from inside your head.

Are you in the U.S.? If so, autism is addressed and protected by the Americans with Disabilities Act (ADA). The ADA guarantees accommodation for your officially diagnosed disability in the classroom, workplace, and anywhere that you could access as a member of the public.

The crappy thing about the ADA is that, although it demands accommodation, it cannot force people to culturally accept or be nice to us. We have to patch those cracks ourselves. Explaining to your boss or teacher that, because you are autistic, you interpret instructions and rules more literally than others should immediately let them know that you are a member of a protected class and that accommodation is their responsibility, not yours. If you are in the U.S. and this does not improve your relationship, you can point out that accommodation is required by law and then politely raise this issue with *their boss*, which usually resolves it quickly, but often harms all of these relationships.

So as to not negatively impact your relationships, explain what you like about the environment as well as what it's like to be you in that environment and why it's difficult. Express your willingness to listen, follow directions, and work hard.

Ultimately, telling people that you're autistic is a road map for the people that you're telling as well. It's an explanation for why they might have different reactions from you than they do from other people. Autism has become increasingly acceptable, so count your blessings. Most of us grew up in the time "before" when we were just seen as difficult, rude, and confrontational in our adherence to rules and response to stimulus.

Lastly and most importantly, coming out to people will tell you who you can trust, who makes you feel good, and who loves you better afterward. It will show other autistic people that it's safe to come forward and that we are everywhere.

Why can't autistic people make eye contact?

Joe again. Being autistic is doing constant emotional labor. We *can* make eye contact, it's just distracting and uncomfortable. It's like how an NT could maintain a polite conversation with a pinched nerve, it's just more difficult to do so and you'd prefer not to. Of course, expectations of eye contact are daily and pinched nerves are less common. Autistic people receive a much greater volume of stimulus all the time, so eye contact causes unease and feels awkward. For some autistic individuals, it's even worse, and looking someone in the eyes is like staring into a lightbulb that burns into our brain.

Often, eye contact just isn't necessary, because it floods autists with information and can overwhelm us. Psychology calls this the Intense World Theory. In short, autistic individuals get information easily and quickly and don't need to maintain eye contact for the purposes that most people do. We also don't get the neuroceptive benefit of eye contact so why force a level of intimacy for no reason? It might feel unnatural to you, or feel like we are lying, or you might suspect some other reason why we cannot look you in the eye. The reality is that many of our mannerisms are different because of the workarounds that we have to create to survive in your world.

I've trained myself to maintain eye contact by going through the motions intellectually. I don't actually look people in the eyes, but I create a similar effect by looking *near* the eyes. I find natural ways to give myself reprieve every few seconds, like picking up a drink, giving a treat to my dog, or gesticulating with my hands, staring into the corner of the room to ponder a question, or writing something down. By maintaining constant motion, I can create some relief for myself without staring at the floor. In environments where eye contact is not expected, I don't need to exert the emotional effort to accommodate the disability of neurotypicals, so I am much more relaxed and not exhausted afterwards.

Do autistic people have problems understanding sarcasm?

OH, TOTALLY. 71 MILLION PEOPLE ON EARTH CANNOT UNDERSTAND SARCASM. Because we are all TOTALLY the same. </ sarcasm>

Humor is an emotional appeal. Autistic people come across as emotionally immature because we express our emotions differently than neurotypicals.

For autists, communication is primarily a form of sharing and exchanging information. But we are a resourceful people and we learn from our experiences and mistakes. So if someone gives us very clear, concrete feedback, we can apply that in very specific ways immediately and learn from it.

This led me (Joe) to a love of puns from a young age and to create word mashups and adopt humor that I'd see elsewhere, mimicking jokes and eventually . . . employing sarcasm.

I work with ASD employees and one of them has a very hard time with humor and sarcasm in middle age. The concepts are clear, but the inflection is hard for them to identify and respond to. It's hard to know *when* someone is being sarcastic. So the sarcasm has to be even more obvious. But once he gets it, he demonstrates this by making several other jokes and wordplay around the original one, often through an email later that day.

Sarcasm is learned for us, albeit at a much slower rate than for neurotypicals. For us, we continue on an intellectual path throughout our lives. Don't give up on someone just because they don't get it right away. With time they'll be walking circles around your piddly sarcastic humor. (Sorry, that last part was sarcastic.)

Do autistic people lie on purpose like neurotypicals do?

Honesty is a very complicated concept for Autistics. We are told to always tell the truth but when someone says, "How are you?" we are expected to lie *every time*. I almost always find people's instructions confusing, misleading, or unnecessarily complicated. "Did you pick up your room?" does not mean "Please move your junk into a pile elsewhere." And "honest" answers become subjective beyond my comprehension.

Similarly, when someone asks us about their appearance, we are really supposed to be cautious in our response. We are supposed to compliment changes in hairstyles and shoes and reduced body mass, even if we don't see these as positive changes. Each time I have not lied on purpose and instead said something like, "Wow, those two colors that you are wearing really don't go together at all," I am treated to harsh stares from the entire room.

In each of these examples, we are told that it's socially proper to lie on purpose, and we don't have the capacity to differentiate harmful lies from polite lies designed to protect the feelings of others (usually called white lies) and lies of omission. I have been told that I am supposed to lie or at least only tell part of the truth when asked for my opinion. The comic *Sandman* plays on this theme when John Dee spends an afternoon in a cafe holding a ruby that forces everyone in his proximity to only tell the truth. Inevitably relationships break down because people aren't prepared for—and largely do not want—the truth. As an autistic person, this was tremendously amusing because it reveals the conflict in offering people the information that they are frequently requesting and how most interactions are variously dishonest theatrical performances.

Naturally, this balance and conflict complicates autistic people's decision-making the rest of the time. Our behavior is a product of our training more than anything else. We don't easily lie maliciously, just like anyone else (who isn't experiencing some serious maladaptive wiring in their brain, or hasn't essentially been taught that lying is the "correct" thing to do when you need to solve a problem). But in general situations (and questions) like this are much more confusing for autistics.

When asked an objective question about facts or experiences, I try to answer honestly, but the question is often not phrased in a manner where the asker can receive the information they wanted, and they end up blaming me.[23] Literally, just about every question that neurotypicals ask has an unclear construction, like "Will you be home at 1 PM for lunch?" could mean "When should I expect you?" or "Are we having lunch together?" or even "I am currently doing salacious things with the mailman and I'd rather that we wrap that up before you get home. Please give me information." Neurotypicals also have this absurd habit of assuming that you don't understand the question if you provide an answer that they do not appreciate or do not expect. E.g., "Are you taking a bath soon?" could mean anything from "You smell and need to do something about that" to "I'm about to consume all of the hot water and I'm trying to masquerade as if I care about your feelings, but I'm actually conveying information under the guise of asking a question." Think about the desired outcome that you are trying to achieve. Simplify the language around it. Make coherent, straightforward requests and you won't get lied to. Every time a neurotypical overcomes their communication disabilities, it inspires us.

---

23 Dr. Faith's *Unfuck Your Friendships: Using Science to Make and Maintain the Most Important Relationships of Your Life* (Microcosm, 2021) has an extensive section on how to talk to neurodiverse friends

What is autistic masking? Does it have repercussions, such as loss of identity?

Starting around six months old, autistic people learn by observation. When we see someone else get an encouraging response to a joke, we believe that we will experience a similar response if we repeat it. This leads to masking. Masking is when an autistic person mimics the clothes, behavior, words, scripts, play, jokes, mannerisms, gestures, or interests of others in an attempt to blend in and go unnoticed among neurotypicals. It's why we repeat our favorite lines from movies or behaviors we see in the world around us. It's why we learn to smile to set other people at ease and feel welcome, even when their manner is stern, upset, or hostile. It's why we make small talk to make others comfortable and feel heard, even though we get nothing out of it. It's why we add inflection to our words, to emphasize meaning. It's why we like to dress like our favorite characters even when it's not Halloween.

Television characters can be our interests but they aren't *us*. Masking is a reproduction of how we see others successfully performing. The problem is that we usually miss important parts of the context or subtext that makes our masking awkward or inappropriately timed, like wearing an anime costume to a job interview.

Once we get a better handle on unobtrusive masking, it quickly becomes "natural" for autistics and we do it without thinking. Unfortunately, we still tend to get fundamental aspects of timing and presentation wrong and it almost never goes well.

Masking is one of the most controversial topics when you engage other autistic people. There are two conflicting schools of thought:

1) Autistic people should learn NT social skills in order to blend and assimilate into society. This will result in less trauma, anxiety, and pain for everyone involved.

2) Autistic assimilation is offensive to its very core. Suppression of our natural state is damaging to our self-image and disconnects us from who we are. We need to be accommodated and understood, not assimilated.

I (Joe) agree with aspects of both of these camps. For one, since social isolation is the principal cause of autistic people being driven to suicide and because of my own experiences with that, I made efforts to learn to socialize and communicate in ways the NTs were expecting. I learned how to make eye contact and add inflection to my voice. I learned how to incorporate humor and figures of speech. I smile and shake hands when I greet people. I perform constant emotional labor to understand what other people are thinking and feeling and experiencing. As a result of this exhausting, humiliating, and tedious process, I am rewarded with endless exclamations of "I can't believe you're autistic!" Worst of all, neurotypicals rarely follow their own rules but somehow get away with it because they have the privilege.

Is it worth it? It's a toss up. I can convincingly be the greatest actor that you've ever seen. But it takes a lot out of me. And again, I'm doing it to placate the imperialists who have the power in this equation. Maybe the worst part is actually that I want them to like me.

But look at it a different way: choosing not to mask is like waiting for the world to change because it "should" accommodate us. It's very likely going to be a lonelier path where you want other people to meet you in the middle because that's the right thing for people to do. However, this is where that deadly social isolation comes from. Most people don't know what autism *is* or how it manifests. Creating that education and awareness is the current step before we can move on to demand acceptance. This is a very lonely place. I agree that we should be accepted. However, I wasn't sure that I'd live long enough to see that happen. So I created a backup plan in the meantime.

Make the choice to mask or not that's right for you. Either way, be aware that masking is exhausting and depleting your precious energy stores. And then you can consciously engage the world with agency—or choose to stay home and decompress.

By establishing and respecting our own personal boundaries, we can surround ourselves with people who are supportive and create the life and world that we want to see. Even if we never need to muster our collective strength, this knowledge will instill us with the confidence to proceed toward our goals.

How has masking affected you?

I (Joe) have masked so fully and deeply for so long that I didn't know my authentic self or who I really was until I was in my

40s. I didn't feel comfortable or safe in my own home until I was 43. It's odd, because so much of my humor, personality, eccentricity, and daily performance were culled from other sources. I don't think that's necessarily uncommon, although the reasons may differ, case by case.

Masking is the autistic performance of behaving like a neurotypical. It includes things like tone of voice, emotional expression, concealing one's true feelings or experience, and expressing one's self inauthentically for others' benefit. Masking is most common in a setting such as a job interview where you are trying to be liked and impress people with your character and abilities. But it also happens at school, at work, at professional conferences, and anywhere that status and emotional experience are a factor.

Similarly, I think about gender as a masking performance. As someone who is autistic, I am expected to look the part of how neurotypicals perceive me. When I am at work, there are different levels of acceptable behavior. When I was a touring speaker from 1997-2017, I had to operate within certain expectations, such as looking at the audience consistently throughout the performance, even though that was uncomfortable for me. I see all these performances the same way as when I played Dungeons & Dragons. I am a character in a costume for various applications. I dress differently today than when I was an electrician, though there was that time that I went straight to the opera after work and couldn't go change. . . .

Sometimes I masked as a character that I enjoyed in a film or a real-life story that resonated with my experience. But mostly I came to realize that I was performing like the people who I had seen receive a positive response. And then, upon receiving a positive response for performing similarly to those people, the mask deepened. I continued to imitate and perform.

Slowly, I lost the distinction of what was me and what was masking. I couldn't figure out at what point my own enjoyment or interest in something began and ended. I liked a positive response and in cases of suicidal ideation and social isolation, to some degree a positive response is important.

But when I got deeper I saw that pleasing others was slowly killing me. My medical doctor pointed it out first: that I didn't actually ever express my own emotions, even in my own ways as an autistic person. She told me to practice expressing my feelings more often.

I had realized that no one wanted to be around an angry, frustrated, upset, or sad person so I stopped performing those feelings and simply internalized them. The difficulty of this is that those feelings are still there. They well up deeper inside of you if you aren't allowed to express them, even if that's simply a self-imposed rule. So I began reincorporating expressing even the smallest emotions—with a fair amount of warning to those closest to me in advance. And gradually I began to return to what anyone might guess is the closest thing possible to my true self.

I will likely turn 60 before I can definitively say which are the authentic parts of myself and which parts are my mask brought about through positive reception from private or public audiences, but I feel better even moving in the correct direction.

As an autistic person, what's something about society that you wish you'd known sooner?

I (Joe) wish I'd known that there isn't one truth. For most NT people, their emotional experience is their reality, rather than the facts of what happened, and both of these things can be "the truth."

I used to subcontract sticker printing work through another print shop. I'd handle sales and service and I'd interface between the customer and the printer. For smaller jobs, the prices were comparable to what a customer would pay going direct. I was always nervous that I would lose my customers if they suspected that they could get better pricing by cutting me out. This created many situations where I had to furiously ride my bike across town to pick up a print job and meet with a customer.

In one case, a band ordered stickers with a fairly tight turnaround because they had a show coming up with the band Blue Oyster Cult. I arranged the timeline with the shop and confirmed with the customer. One day, I got a phone call from the customer. They wanted to swing by and see if the stickers were ready for pickup. I should have said "Sorry, not yet." but instead I told them that the printing warehouse was pretty confusing to navigate and that I'd prefer it if she swung by my house that evening to pick them up instead.

I hit a nerve. "I'm a delivery person for UPS so I navigate difficult buildings every day. I don't appreciate the insinuation that I'm not smart enough to figure out a print shop. Is it because I'm a woman? Why do you want me to come to your house anyway?"

She interpreted my effort to maintain a boundary between my services and the shop as sexism. I tried to insist I was trying to be helpful but the story was fishy enough so I fessed up that I brokered through a print shop. She didn't order again and didn't let go of the belief that I thought women were not smart enough to navigate a warehouse. To her, it appeared like I was lying even though I did confess and eventually told her the complete truth.

In another case, I was leaving work and happened to run into a friend outside. My friend and I talked casually for an hour before I went back in to retrieve something that I forgot from my office. A co-worker who was perpetually annoyed with me found my reappearance in the office somehow to be suspicious. I explained that I had run into a friend and had then remembered something that I forgot, so I came back for it. She narrowed her eyes and said "I think you are up to something." I was dreadfully confused. I was telling the truth. And the truth didn't even seem implausible or strange. She knew that my friend lived a block away and I often ran into her in this neighborhood.

Gradually, I came to understand that, regardless of the facts, people will have different perspectives on the events that they witness. Arguing and trying to explain the facts or my position isn't going to make people agree with me; it only makes things worse.

How people feel (which is often a result of past interactions with other people in their lives) dictates their perspective and lived experience. This is why arguing about tangible details with them is only going to hurt you both. In both cases, I should have apologized instead of trying to explain away misunderstandings. Their feelings and realities were starkly out of touch with my motives but that didn't matter. Their emotional experience was telling them a different story and bringing in facts felt like a renewed effort to undermine reality.

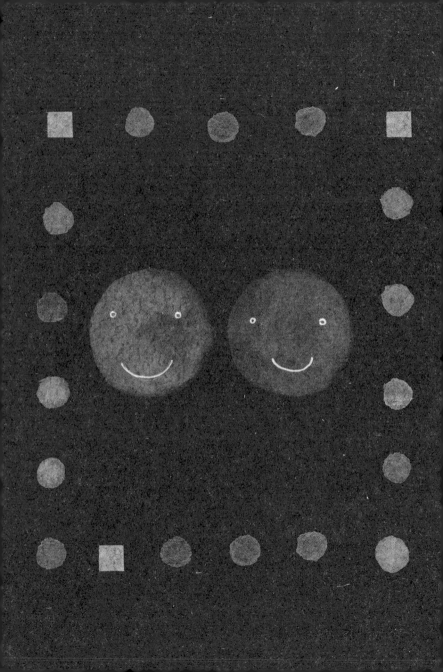

HOW DO I NAVIGATE FRIENDSHIP, RELATIONSHIPS, AND DATING?

These are pretty complicated. Fortunately, we have two entire, separate books about this, *Autism Relationships Handbook: How to Thrive in Friendships, Dating, and Love* and *Autism Relationships Workbook: How to Thrive in Friendships, Dating, and Love*. Both have been very popular and even a group of "pickup artists"[24] said that if you look past our blue hair and "social justice writing," we have lots of good information. So if people who diametrically oppose our political and moral stances can find value in our work, we truly believe that anyone can. For the record, neither of us have blue hair, but it was an interesting idea to consider for a few seconds.

What are the main problems and solutions that autistic people have in friendships and relationships?

Most of my (Joe's) adult relationships mirrored how I was raised as a child. I was frequently insulted and told that I was "stupid" for not understanding basic "truths" about the world. I once lived with a chef who relentlessly mocked my inability to cook more than the same few meals for myself. The only reason that I had learned or been able to cook at all is because I worked in food service from the time that I was fourteen as a

---

24 Sexist "men's rights" groups who have created elaborate systems to manipulate women into sleeping with them.

means of supporting myself. I learned to cook in an industrial environment and then scaled it back to a single or double portion. I learned at age 40 that I only knew how to scramble eggs like a short-order cook. In many ways, things like cooking or making my bed were deeply tied to the trauma of my youth and how others angrily mocked me for not being like them. As a result, I prefer restaurants to cooking for myself, because the experience makes me feel like I've achieved a pillar of success.

In the Netflix series *Atypical* we watch protagonist Sam engage in some bumbling transitions into adulthood [spoiler alert]. We watch him fall in love with his therapist, the first person that he has a truly intimate adult relationship with outside of his nuclear family. He mistakes this intimacy as mutual love and attempts to break into her home to impress her with an aphrodisiac. The results are painful and predictable but amusing. Sam is confused and wants to continue seeing her as his therapist and does not understand why this is unacceptable. He is tricked out of money and mocked when he cannot understand that other kids are making fun of him. He takes people at their word and face value in ways that all autistic people are prone to. He develops an actual relationship and then learns the hard lesson that you don't tell someone that you aren't in love with them in front of their entire extended family. Those are the kinds of rules that an autistic person historically only learned through painful mistakes. I have a similar encyclopedia of stories about stupid things that I've done while following the rules as they were explained to me. This doesn't have to be the case and my partner and I are doing increasingly better at being proactive instead of reactive with the people we love.

Fortunately, in the US and most of the UK and Europe, the law is on our side. We are afforded reasonable accommodation under the Americans with Disabilities Act and are seen as a "vulnerable population," as we are legally regarded as developmentally disabled people. However, this only protects us from discrimination from institutions, not individuals. So if we get kicked out of a 7-11 for stimming, i.e., "being weird," that's discrimination. Often I'm too exhausted to advocate for myself alone until an issue is resolved. Fortunately, I've surrounded myself with people that I can trust. They do a tremendous job of standing up to stupidity and making a case around the facts.

For most autistic people, this is not how things turn out. They are sheltered from the world for fear that they will make mistakes or get hurt. But life is a product of making a series of mistakes and learning from them. Sure, those mistakes hurt, but they are certainly better than living with your abusive or coddling parents for the rest of your life.

The thing that helps autistic people be part of a relationship and conversation is when someone can step back, drop the assumptions, and use more basic language. I needed help communicating with my former partners about needs and expectations and wants. Autistic people need someone to make sure that we understand before proceeding or assuming that we are being "difficult." My partner now is very good about meeting me halfway. I still have to frequently look up words to find out what they mean but then she instructs me on the finer points of what they *actually mean* since apparently the meanings in the dictionary are not the ones that most people intend.

Several people in my ASAN group said that they learned how to be a person in the world by working in retail before their diagnosis. Yes, it was exhausting, terrible torture but it taught them the basics of interacting with people, solving problems, and getting their needs met. And they understand that they don't have to continue being traumatized from being subjected to still working in the retail environment now. One woman in my ASAN group explained that she learned life skills by running away from sociopathic parents and joining a religious cult for several years. She found that being in close quarters with other people where certain tasks must be performed as a team was difficult but taught her how to have a conversation and take care of herself in life.

The risk here is not letting other people dictate our lives and priorities. When I was married in my mid-20s, I came to accept and defer to others' depiction of what was "normal" and their expectations for my behavior and opinions. My truth and feelings and personality were slowly overwritten and I lost myself. I came to realize how painful and damaging that was for me and eventually got out of that dynamic. I now have had a partner for thirteen years who is supportive and understanding of my gaffes and the fact that I still see no logical reason to ever make my bed (Hard agree on this point. –Faith) and still misuse words because I'm an autodidact.

Still, it takes a special person to embrace an autistic person without trying to "make us a better person," but to accept us as we are. We will embarrass the people who love us. We take up a lot of emotional and mental space. We take up a lot of time. But we respond with kindness, loyalty, and honesty. Everyone wants a friend that you can give a specific day and time to, months away, and say "I need you to show up with 50 chairs, a shovel, and a pet chinchilla." We're those people. We just need clarification on what color chinchilla you're seeking.

How can you talk to an autistic person?

Face the person that you want to address and use your mouth to create words in their native language. If you are unfamiliar with their native language, it's okay to ask. At least for starters, it's best to avoid metaphors, sarcasm, and jokes until you have a feel for each other.

More than anything, do not condescend. We are smart; probably smarter than you. I mean, here you are asking for advice about communication. Ironic, huh? So spare us the superiority. We get enough of it elsewhere, I assure you. Show us respect and patience. Sometimes it'll take lots of patience, but the reason for that is partially your fault for not historically following the above directions.

Communicate in terms of goals rather than in terms of directions. For example, say: "if you prevent your shoelaces from touching the ground, your shoes will be more comfortable and last longer because they won't come untied," rather than "tie your shoes."

I find it utterly baffling when someone expresses a need to discuss a matter on the telephone and they waste fifteen minutes of my time by talking about nothing, in a vain effort to make themselves feel comfortable to say what they need to, in some misplaced fear that they might upset me. But this is how I accommodate neurotypical needs on a daily basis. Not that I like it.

Sometimes, autistics are what is referred to as nonverbal or "language light." This is not to be confused with an inability to understand things. We are always observing—usually too much and more than we would like—and we can still understand what you are expressing. Other times, it's emotionally overwhelming and it takes us a little bit to muster and structure the response that we intend. Or you might encounter various character performances from our years of masking and attempting to fit into society. Patience is necessary.

We may understand your words in ways you never intended. The mother of an autistic boy told me that her son was terrified that she would eat him when she referred to him as "a sweet boy" because the other things she'd referred to as "sweet" were eaten until nothing was left. He was worried for his future fate and brought up this concern for weeks afterwards.

Lastly, show us love. Asking specific questions is best. Don't tell us how to be or what to do. Accept that we are people and can make our own choices. We'll be honest with you, so get ready for that. We can even cultivate the kind of loving, yet biting feedback that some people don't want to hear. We say it because we care about you, not because we are trying to get under your skin or manipulate you. We want emotional proximity just like you but it's a bit more of a challenge for us. We're too busy building spaceships in our heads and counting tiles and obsessing over stuff that's really cool. You probably wouldn't understand but that's okay. We still do our best to respect you and we'd be happy to explain it to you if you'd like.

When someone says "I like you," what are you supposed to do if you are autistic and don't know how to deal with emotions?

The good news is that it's the same when someone likes an autistic person as it is for everyone else.

Step one: Determine if you are interested in them and/or like them. If you aren't interested, it's okay to return a vague compliment ("Oh, I think you are great too!") but don't express specific romantic interest. If you want to give an explicit rejection, you could say something like "Thank you! I'm not looking to date right now but I'm incredibly flattered!"

If you are interested in pursuing things further, let them know! Offer a big smile and compliment specific aspects of their personality or personal style that genuinely reflect your views. Don't stare or prolong the encounter. Ask them if they'd like to do something with you outside of your usual time together and exchange phone numbers.

If things are unclear, ask clarifying questions. E.g., "Thanks. I think that you're wonderful too. Do you mean that you like me as a friend or perhaps as more than a friend?"

When someone expresses romantic interest, it's a rare moment where it's okay to compliment their appearance ("I think you're really cute!"). Don't be too specific when talking about their body. We know, the allistics do it all the time. But our physical bodies are something we don't have a lot of control over, so focus on the things that they do have control over. Compliment choices that they made to express themselves and their personalities, especially in a non-gendered way (like not handsome or beautiful . . . any words we associate with specific genders). What do we mean by that?

> No: You have the prettiest green eyes! *(Thanks, but I was born with them, didn't pick them up at Target last week so.....?)*

> Also no: You're eyeshadow makes your eyes look so gorgeous *(Erm, thanks, but I'm nonbinary, so I'm not super comfortable with the word gorgeous)*

> Yes!: Your eye makeup is on-point, you look amazing! *(There we go!)*

Remember details about them and your encounters to mention again later. E.g., "Remember that funny thing we both saw?" Be consistent and solid but don't chase them too hard or linger in their personal space too early in the relationship. Keep things organic and let them develop naturally and gradually. Relationships blossom better when both parties are a little nervous and excited rather than when there is pressure to do things or stress.

Step two: Escalate. If there's mutual good feelings from both of you, continue to spend more time together and participate in more activities that bond you two. Take an emotional inventory: do they make you feel good more often than they make you feel bad? If you're unsure about how they feel, ask them about it. Something like, "How do you feel about how things are going between us? Is there something that I could do differently to make you feel better about things?"

Step three: Ask for permission and check in. A lot of times NT relationships fizzle because people don't know how to talk about their feelings. As an ASD individual, you have a strong advantage here because you are forced to navigate your feelings and responses much more actively than an NT. Most people might get a little uncomfortable when prompted to talk about their feelings. But in the long run, they will appreciate it much more than having not discussed it, even if it's awkward in the moment.

Despite what you might see on TV or in movies, most people do not like to be abrasively kissed or groped out of nowhere. Even if that's someone's kink, that should be established and boundaried ahead of time. And you have a strong advantage here again as you can set and follow rules better than most people. Check in frequently, especially when escalating in a romantic or intimate situation. It doesn't have to be weird and stilted and a buzz kill. It can be really sexy to say *"You have to tell me what you want or I'm not gonna do it"* in a low and soft, performative voice right? If you are annoying the person, they will likely say something once sufficient trust has been established. Because you have demonstrated that you respect them, they will feel that they can ask you for what they need and vice versa.

This person likes you and is invested in you, so don't betray that trust. Be honest, and they will continue to assume your best intentions.

I like someone who likes me back but we have never talked to each other. We are both shy. Should I make a move? How?

Since you know that you like each other even though you haven't talked, I assume that you have some reliable third parties providing second-hand information.

Everyone craves attention from the people that they enjoy spending time with. *Everyone.* You have to obtain some basic information about them. What does they enjoy doing and talking about? What is their sense of humor like?

A fairly surefire way of doling out attention is to deliver a well-intentioned compliment and then offer a prolonged smile. The situation may become awkward but the risk is minimal since you've already established that you both have interest.

Ask if they might want to spend time with you somewhere that you don't normally see each other. Maybe ask them to watch a movie with you or drink tea or go to a party or come with you to a friend's house.

From there, build gradually. Tell them that you had a nice time if that is true. Ask them to do it again. Communicate and ask what each of you like and don't like before someone has committed a faux pas. Ask clarifying questions, like "You say that you don't like parties, but you went to Cheryl's anyway?

What motivated you to attend? Was it fun for you?" Questions like these, when asked and answered honestly, create a firmer understanding of each other's character, interests, and behavior. Gradually, they become increasingly normal conversations and continue to escalate.

It will be awkward at first, but you'll master it in no time!

An autistic guy kissed me. Was it his disorder or does he actually like me?

A person with an allistic disorder received a kiss. Is it their disorder that makes this gesture unclear to them, or are they unsure if they share mutual interest?

I am always flummoxed that even when autistic people perform NT-style emotional expression, we are still pathologized. Hopefully he asked if it was okay before moving in for the big kiss, or received confirmation of mutual interest, but I can't really see any interpretation of why you would kiss someone who you didn't actually like.

Sure, sometimes the motives are rather nebulous between "lusty physical attraction seeking hookup" versus "wow, I want to spend the rest of my life with this wonderful person." And sure, some people are much more interested in the former while verbally expressing interest in the latter. So these are the questions that one must really pursue and evaluate relevant data from. Yes, I do also understand that those fluttering feelings of new love are so overwhelming that they prompt doubt and confusion. But really, when someone kisses you, the first question your brain asks is "Does he actually like me?" and it's not rhetorical?

As an autistic person, are you happier in a relationship with another autistic person, or with a neurotypical?

I've mostly only dated NTs and when I did date an autistic person for a very short time, her behavior was unfamiliar to me. It wasn't how I had taught myself to relate and socialize so instead of being comforting, it was confusing. I am fairly certain that I dated several Borderline Personality Disorder individuals, but my inability to see the dynamics of the situation and relationships plus my lack of boundaries prevented me from seeing how unhealthy this was. I was thinking the other day about another short relationship where someone stalked me and eventually dumped me because I was incapable of emotionally relating on the necessary levels—a concept that I was yet unfamiliar with. Regardless of the specifics and whether the other person acted appropriately or not, it was very difficult for me to understand and process where each person was coming from.

So the necessary step was getting my act together. In therapy, I spent years unpacking the first 30 years of my own life, experiences, behaviors, reactions, and relational dynamics and then putting it back together to understand why these outcomes had been occurring. This process required about four years of intensively focusing on things I had been oblivious to or ignored. And then the pieces came together.

Now I've been in a relationship for thirteen years with someone who is much less relational and much more logical, though still NT. This makes it much easier to relate and express feelings while still being able to have reasoned conversations. I am allowed to react and be myself, which is honored and respected. We mutually share experiences and divide tasks in a way that honors our respective needs and abilities. We can openly discuss relationship dynamics in ourselves and what we observe in the world around us to make our relationship better and it's highly rewarding. I have no regrets.

I think it would be really special to have a relationship with an autist, someone who could truly understand what I go through and how "basic" things become excruciating or incredibly difficult. It wouldn't require the levels of exposition that I've spent a dozen years on. However, that isn't what the cards drew for me. Pending disaster, this is likely going to be the relationship that I'm in for the long haul. And it's sort of a meeting in the middle on this issue without anyone feeling like their compromise is dramatic.

So, as an autist, I think it's important not to draw a hard line in the sand. Be in a relationship with the person you relate to and who makes you happy, whether they are NT or ASD. Love the person, not the neurotype.

Is it difficult for autistic people to take accountability? How can I negotiate relationship conflict?

Sadly, I (Joe) think the answer is "yes." Not because we are stubborn assholes who are never apologetic and want to repair harm, but because we often struggle with the distinction between "intent" and "impact." It's very complex for us to understand that we can hurt other people's feelings while trying to help them and do the right thing.

When we hurt someone, our cognitive instinct is to explain our actions, intents, and goals. To most NTs, this comes across as being argumentative or, worse, diminishing the legitimacy of their feelings.

The primal difference between the two brain types is the difference between an emotional, narrative truth for an NT and a rational, cognitive series of events for an autistic person. For the NT, their experience is summarized by how they feel in the moment and that truth overrides all other factors. Even if there is nothing they can point to, their brain will access their feelings and tell them stories about their experience. This conflicts sharply with the autistic brain, which is forever seeking facts and evidence for its theses and best practices determinations, asking *why did that happen?*

It's hard for us to accept accountability because we don't feel like we did anything wrong. Rather than looking at how we hurt someone, our narrative is what we were attempting to do. It took me until my 30s to understand that my perceptions are not the same as someone else's. And slowly from there, I was able to unpack a lifetime of experiences. Of why people were upset with me, and how a series of what to me feels like unrelated events create a tapestry of experiences for others.

After getting my legs underneath me and understanding these concepts, I began mentoring half a dozen autistic people. One by one, they wanted to discuss situations where they were "wronged." They wanted to figure out how to "make" the other person do something or understand something. I felt sad for them. We dug through the facts. In each case, the issue was invariably that they had hurt someone else and felt hurt when that person reacted harshly. One man in his 50s went as far as saying "I don't hurt people. I help people." His self image was such that he could not accept that he had hurt someone because that wasn't how he viewed himself.

In each of these cases (and my own), the appropriate response was to listen to the issues surrounding the conflict and take responsibility for and learn from the ways that our actions affect other people unintentionally. Then we can apologize for the hurt and difficulty that we caused and move on with our lives. It's the tendency of all people to point to the most absurd and baseless accusations, rather than the ones that have merit. We try to paint our own innocence rather than take responsibility. Some accusations won't fit but let's focus on the ones that do.

We won't resolve every dispute but creating closure for ourselves and enabling our learning curve helps us to grow from these conflicts rather than seeing them as a series of unrelated events. We can make other people feel better.

Conflicts are never one-sided though. In a conflict, talk about how the other person's behavior impacted your feelings. Then take a turn discussing how your behavior impacted the other person's feelings. Do nothing but listen during these moments of sharing and do not interrupt. Don't think about nuances that make their statements incorrect. Think about how they can perceive these things to be true. Put your thoughts and feelings together when you are alone and really figure out how you would like to be treated and how the way that they are treating you now makes you feel. The most helpful script that I learned was "When you do this, I feel like this." It works like magic.

Honestly share your experiences and what it's like to be you. Explain what they could do that would be helpful to you. For example, I find clear, actionable instructions for what is expected of me to be very helpful.

For example, saying, "Meet me outside in five minutes so we can leave together," as opposed to, "We're all in the car," makes a world of difference for an autist even if others assume that the rest is nonverbally communicated. Find a way to say what you mean without implicit assumptions. The real problem isn't that I wasn't listening, it's that you hadn't connected your concepts. You can blame me or we can solve the problem.

In a romantic relationship, express in no uncertain terms what you need out of the relationship. Tell them what you love about them and what attracted you in the first place. Then again express what you need. Be specific and concrete

("I want to have date night at least twice per week and it better be romantic, mathdammit!").

Sharing our feelings and experience honestly strengthens our relationships. I've found that telling stories to trustworthy neurotypicals helps them to better relate with us and better understand people that they love who are on the spectrum.

These conflicts can feel constant and inevitable but by listening and being open to other people's point of view without letting it erase our own, we can show that we respect them and are capable of solving problems together. Always think of any conflict as the two of you against the problem. That way everyone can get what they need and some of what they want as well!

How far does autism go as an excuse or explanation for physically or verbally hurting someone? When do you draw the line between abusive and autistic?

Autism is never an excuse for behavior that harms another person. Trying to explain away the responsibility of your actions because of your autism will only lead to hurt, isolation, and the other parties feeling guilty for having their feelings hurt.

Nineteen years ago I didn't know how to get what I needed or wanted and accepted that I just couldn't or wouldn't. When my partner at the time began sleeping with other people and coming home blackout drunk (despite my protestations), it ceased to resemble a relationship. She belittled me on a daily basis and I realized there wasn't anything left to stick around for. In hindsight, she didn't know how to manage or navigate or even talk about my autism. It was scary and traumatic, but I had a few supportive people in my life and without them I'm sure that I would be dead in a ditch.

Autistics learn by trying, failing, and trying again based on feedback from others and any data that is available. Much of anyone's personality is formed during childhood. Being raised by people with their own unresolved issues causes any child, autistic or otherwise, to maladapt, or to attempt to manage their problems through mishandling power or using methods for getting by in the world that may not work outside of their nuclear family. A child raised like this will often grow up into someone who tries to control others to get their wants satisfied.

Left undiagnosed for any period into adulthood, autistic people tend to create maladaptive workarounds for attempting to get their wants met based on bad habits they picked up in childhood or in their family of origin. e.g. If one parent belittled the other and got what they wanted, the outcome is noted, not the cost. These recursive tendencies are the autist trying to get by in the world not built for us.

We are more likely to be on the receiving end of abuse than to be doling it out. I have been accused of being emotionally abusive—especially boundary violations—during a time in my life when I was not able to interpret people's emotional communication. So, I am sympathetic to the complexity of the situation on both sides. It's important for an autist to feel understood and respected but this can be exhausting when the other party's feelings are hurt.

A support system for everyone involved, is absolutely essential for recovery during times of conflict as we cannot shame people into functional adaptive systems. We have to love and trust them to love us. In many cases, your partner may be suffering from recursion, learned behavior that they thinks will solve problems based on ways that power has been taken away throughout their life.

That said, solving the problem might not be your role. And you might need to get out if your relationship is not emotionally safe. You two might have too much history. You might have already emotionally departed the relationship and have nothing more to give. They could be struggling in ways that might be beyond your skills and capacity. It may be up to them to find someone else who understands them and can work with them. Individual therapy is probably a good idea for both of you.

If one partner is older, more experienced, or has more privileges in society, there's a power dynamic at play in your relationship. On top of that, if you've been dating them since you were a teenager (as is frequently the case in questions posed to Joe), that kind of power divide is destructive to the fabric of a relationship without some careful mindfulness from the older person. And that can be difficult to convince the more privileged person to take seriously, because they've always benefited from it—consciously or not!

If you think the relationship might be salvageable, establish some quantitative and clear demands. Autists do well with clear instructions. Be sympathetic to their experiences and difficulties in your demands. You want this because it's what's best for them and you see what's difficult.

1) If you're going to stay in this relationship, they need to understand what motivates their behavior and find better coping strategies for getting what they want and need. This may be a diagnosis, therapy, or social skills training. But they need to get out of maladaptive coping to get what they want.

2) Autism is not an excuse. It's a toolkit and roadmap. So don't let them be an asshole about it. Sure, their demons are fierce and intense. But that doesn't let them off the hook. If they're going to be in a relationship, that's a two-way street. They need to make you feel loved and listened to.

3) Create a standard of accountability so that you are both happy in the relationship and their behaviors can be managed and kept in check.

4) Explain that abuse and threats only drive you away. These actions come from a place of very low self-esteem. Autism is already hell on relationships but it's worsened with maladaptive coping mechanisms. Tell them that you believe that they can do better and you see these as their worst behaviors and not indicative of their true self or personality.

5) That is, if you want that. If you don't love them anymore even if they could recover, you need to create a clean exit strategy and move on.

So while being an autistic person without proper coping skills can often lead to verbal or physical hurt, that doesn't excuse the behavior; it only explains how it feels like someone's only hope. Most important, it's not your responsibility to fix someone else, only to take care of yourself.

Do autistic people miss people they stop interacting with?

Sure, though like many things, our emotional expression and habits might not be the same as NT people.

Just this week, I had an interaction with someone I knew previously in my life. He was the first person that I had purchased an original painting from and hung it on my wall when I achieved the disposable income to do that. I had supported and promoted and published his work for years before he shifted gears and disavowed himself from his previous work to teach and write fiction. I sent him a congratulatory message about a new publishing deal for his work. I meant it sincerely. It would benefit people's ability to find and enjoy his work.

He interpreted my note as sarcastic, condescending, and insulting. Somehow, my sincerity felt like a biting jab instead. Thinking about it a day later, I realized that this was probably a product of my message coming out of the blue after so many years of not having a proper sit down conversation like we used to. Perhaps, as he becomes more successful in some ways, other creatives feel the need to be competitive or respond with "clever" insults. It was revealing for me about the reasons why so many people never respond when I get in touch again many years after the fact. It hurt, obviously, because it was difficult to understand why his gut reaction was to assume that I would mean to punch down at him after so many years of support. Again, this was probably related to how other people have treated him over the years, which makes it a sad disconnect for both of us.

Many people that I have previously known or been close to in my life have gone on to certain amounts of fame so it's unlikely that they will create time to socialize with me as we did ten or twenty years ago. I don't long for people when we are apart or feel an emotional compulsion to share their company again. But I miss someone quite a bit more if they reject me, especially for ill-conceived or factually inaccurate reasons.

In many ways, I appreciate what we have. Because I don't think of it as over. I still have those experiences and memories and I don't need further interactions to fill any kind of void. Socializing is a prickly mess that is infinitely complicated. I have so many social opportunities and people in my daily life now, and I don't keep in touch with people who are unavailable, even though I think fondly of them.

At the same time, it's common for me to get back in touch with someone twenty years later to send a positive word and resume where we left off. Often, I am surprised and confused to discover that someone is remarkably changed and has new interests and behaviors. Because to me, until shown otherwise, they are right where I left them with the same relationship that we had before. In reality, their adult lives have moved on and it may be difficult to relate with how we have progressed and evolved differently.

As an autistic person, has anybody ever called you selfish or said that you don't care about anybody but yourself?

When I was seventeen, I had a job where I earned a lot of money. I was dating a nineteen year old who worked part time in a bar. Two weeks into our relationship, we went past a restaurant and she, somewhat jokingly, demanded that I buy her dinner. We were heading to her house, where she, an adult, was going to eat dinner. So I declined . . . perhaps too dismissively. For the remainder of our relationship, she called me "selfish." This confused me because I knew what selfishness was. It's a lack of concern for others. Demanding that I buy dinner for her at a time when it was neither necessary or practical, when there was no implicit need at all, was not a product of my supposed selfishness. It was a product of my problem-solving mind.

As a teenager, it was easy to imprint upon my self-image. Was I selfish? Now, I lack a high school education and find myself frequently looking up the meaning of words in order to make sure that I am using them correctly. The denotation of many words fall far from how these words are used in practice or conversation. Often the connotation of those words adds depths of meaning that is lost on me. When I declared to a room that my friend was infamous, I didn't understand why everyone laughed. He had created a public scandal by revealing the inner workings of public schools.

For autistic people, it's difficult to understand what other people are thinking or feeling unless they tell us in plain, exact language or we have a lot of history together. For some reason, most people are very uninclined to do either of these things and instead get upset that we can't figure it out.

A few years before the incident with my then-girlfriend, a friend demanded that I loan him five dollars so that he could purchase the tape that he wanted from the record store. I declined. He insisted that he would pay me back when we got back to our neighborhood. I told him that I might need that cash later that night for something else. He got so pissed at me that this incident eroded our friendship forever. We still hung out but we absolutely lacked the emotional proximity that we had previously. Was I being "selfish?" Well, I had considered his request and declined it on the chance that it might limit my choices later. Perhaps I should have offered more exposition to show the inner workings of my process and that I had considered his request before declining him.

It was my money that I had earned from my job. I had a concern for him but didn't think that waiting another day or two to buy the tape would hurt him. Besides, if he had money at home, why hadn't he brought it for such an important purchase? I can see how he saw it as rude and upsetting but I don't think it was selfish and it definitely felt overstated when he distanced our friendship over it. But it was likely that what seemed like an isolated incident to me was likely what he saw as a pattern in my behavior. I now understand that others are allowed to see me differently than I see myself.

Is it oppressive to want an autistic friend to empathize, validate, or acknowledge your feelings more?

Joe here. Autistic adults are probably doing all of these things, albeit perhaps in a form of verbal or emotional processing that you cannot interpret. We hear your feelings, though it can sometimes be harder or take longer to access other people's feelings as we are often overwhelmed. While it's harder for us to reach empathy and connect other people's emotional states to our own, that can make the impact much greater when I can finally relate to someone's emotional state. My mirror neurons are particularly weak so when I inadvertently cause hurt, connecting my feeling of remorse is mostly a reverse-engineering of thought processes instead of an emotive gut punch. I also remember all of my emotional failings in unfortunate amounts of detail which is certainly a lot of baggage to carry around. Honestly, unpacking it, figuring out what went wrong, and trying to learn from those mistakes is as effective a coping strategy as any I've discovered. I am no longer in regular social skills training but I do have a few psych professionals that I can ask about things like, "Is this person being weird or am I being weird?" and that helps. Talking it over with other autistics is great coping as well.

Honestly, your friend probably just needs clearer instruction. They most likely want to perform the duties of being your friend, at least as best as they are capable. But sometimes it's back to basics training, like "When I tell you how I feel, I want you to repeat that back to me in your own words. This helps me to know that you heard me and understand the intensity of those experiences for me. I understand that your experience is different. Let's practice a few samples now."

Achieving your desired outcome is possible but it requires a lot of trust and patience on both ends. Their probably deficits in theory of mind make it difficult for them to relate their own feelings and experience to yours. They are simultaneously swimming in so many thoughts and feelings that it can create an overwhelming static jet engine. So your ASD friend will likely fall down a few distractions and tangents on their way to empathizing and validating your feelings. They may get stuck on their own feelings a few times on the way there too.

Perhaps the hardest thing for you to accept and understand is that this may be too difficult for them at this time. It's very frustrating to be told to simply try harder. That's not a coherent instruction for us. We need to be walked along neural pathways and trains of thought in regions of the brain where there are a lot of connecting trains. This doesn't mean that the person doesn't love and care for you; it just means that it may not feel that way to you all the time and their apparent word salad can hurt your feelings.

I've been in relationships where I can empathize well enough with my partner that I have mathematical formulas to predict their emotional outcomes and timelines consistently. While this could come across as insultingly intellectual to the wrong person, most appreciate this as a knowledge well. I can predict when an estranged person will get back in touch or who will heal their hurt feelings in time. I can predict how long suffering will last and do understand and acknowledge feelings, though I've definitely offended people and bulldozed boundaries by being oblivious and patronizing over the years. It has been a decades-long process.

For your case, it's a matter of showing them how valuable this connection can be and building trust mutually towards this goal. Perhaps explain that this is what is important to you and work from there.

HOW DO WE CONCLUDE THIS BOOK?

Does media representation matter?

In 2017 *Sesame Street* introduced its first new muppet in a decade. Julia is a four-year-old autistic character who likes painting and picking flowers. On the show you watch Julia's clumsy attempts to mask by repeating the other characters. Big Bird has trouble getting her attention and the other characters learn from Julia.

After launching the new character on the show, the parent company polled 1,000 families about its impact. And the findings were incredible: families with autistic children feel more comfortable incorporating them into broader community activities because of the character and families without autistic children are more accepting of them because of Julia. One autistic five-year-old read a *Sesame Street* book with her mother to understand her diagnosis and at the end she asked her mom "So I'm amazing too, right?"

To understand how much impact Julia had, consider three 2017 studies that found that neurotypical peers are less willing to interact with autistic people based on "thin slice judgments." NTs make judgments and perceptions that result in subconscious decisions not to socialize with us. This is not because of our personalities or actions. It's because of how they "read" us. Within seconds, they see us as "less favorable" due to a range of traits and they are less inclined to pursue social interaction. These biases disappear when the interaction is reduced to only conversational content without our mannerisms. Think about that for a second. It's not our substance; it's their prejudice. It's the ultimate microaggression!

Clearly if Julia can solve this problem so cleanly and easily by simply explaining autism to a general audience of children and families, imagine what the world might look like with a general understanding and acceptance of autistic people. There's a new movement to create a cultural identity around being autistic that interests me. I (Joe) relate with autistic people as "my people." They live with and experience hardship and prejudice in the same way that I do. I ran into one woman who refers to autistics as an "ethnic minority." I think it's an interesting concept but even a year later, I'm not sure how I feel about it. What I do know is that we need a pride movement if we are going to create the kind of awareness that Julia has been so that we can survive past 36 years old and dig in to build lives around our own meaning and purpose.

Is autism strictly a choice?

Yes, autism is strictly a choice.

Autism presents every bystander with the choice of whether or not to be empathic and understanding, or doubting, selfish, discriminating, and pathologizing.

At least every few weeks, and whenever I go somewhere by myself, people talk very slowly in simple speech to me, seat me furthest away from the front of any establishment, and treat me as incapable of understanding even the most basic concepts. Once, when scheduling an interview for an entrepreneurism podcast, after I stated my availability, the producer proceeded to explain how time zones work to me. They included narration on the program that they were surprised how good I was at understanding and talking about business concepts. I was not treated equitably with other guests.

Once, boarding the city bus, a driver explained that I could pay a lower fare, based solely on my appearance. Once, walking around DC, a stranger told me that I wasn't capable of taking care of myself. Those assumptions were all choices made by other people about how to judge and communicate with and about me.

Fortunately, more and more people are taking the time to understand autistic people and respect us. But it is painful, difficult, and a resounding wound every time someone chooses to say something insulting to an autistic person.

We just have different brains that lead us to make choices differently. It shouldn't be that difficult for you to understand this and make the choice to respect us, but we understand that you have certain limitations in your neurotype. For this reason, we find you inspiring every day.

Why do some people think it's cool to be autistic?

Autism advocacy of the past 30 years has focused intensely on the rights and struggles of parents. This has largely resulted in the current movement of invisibly disordered adults who have little voice or understanding of what they are going through.

For an "incurable disorder," we are presented with three options in life:

1. Commit suicide (remember, this is our most likely cause of death until we turn 37)

2. Live anxiously and awkwardly in random efforts to conform and blend (remember, this is typically the cause of above)

3. Have pride in who we are: embracing ourselves and rejecting other people's depictions and judgments of our value in society.

I tried #1 and #2 and found that #3 was by far the best choice, though it took me until my mid-30s to really figure that out. I also tried to isolate myself socially on a (metaphorical) desert island, but that just pushed me back towards #1. Now, I firmly believe that a pride movement is our only way forward to preventing the murder-by-suicide rules that society imposes on us, you know?

Surviving through all of this crap has made me full of grit, incredibly stubborn, and intent on demonstrating a more sustainable path for my fellow autists.

If we take nothing else away from this book, what should we remember?

Since neurotypicals hold the power, they set the standards, but this doesn't mean our needs are secondary, even if they are treated that way. Most framing of autism as a "disability" is actually a result of how the world operates and a lack of accommodation for us. Still, that doesn't mean that there is anything wrong with being autistic. Labeling someone "high functioning" or "low functioning" is to misunderstand the three-dimensional nature of that space and only serves to isolate them or deny them the support that they need.

We experience far greater sensory perception than neurotypicals, which can be a blessing and sometimes feel like a curse. Our charms and merits aren't always going to be appreciated, but we can create scripts for complicated social situations and practice in advance.

Look at the nuance. Learn to recognize and acknowledge other people's different experiences. They will remember and interpret situations differently than you do and that's a good thing. Be responsible for your own actions and take feedback, even if it doesn't align with how you see yourself. Sort out any kernels of truth from even the wildest accusations.

We are stronger together as a community, but that doesn't mean that all autistic people are the same or even agree on everything. Still, we face a common struggle to be respected and accepted. A key means to that end is using our ability to look at solutions to problems differently. A study at the Autism Research Centre tested 600,000 neurotypicals and 30,000 autistic people and learned that autistic people are far more likely to be inventors and work in engineering fields due to our talents for hyper-systematizing. We seek and detect patterns in our natural environment so we are naturally better at observing them—and solving the problems systematically.

Having perspective on your own life and experiences is a powerful first step. Finding your meaning and purpose and clinging to it for dear life are a great way to find your people and ensure your longevity and know your value.

You won't always need to wear a mask. Your future is unwritten.

WHAT ELSE SHOULD WE READ?

Most books about autism are sadly disappointing or already outdated. There are also many memoirs on the subject, but as far as books to help with your situation and understand the history, there are a few more:

- *Neurotribes: The Legacy of Autism and the Future of Neurodiversity* by Steve Silberman

- *The Autism Relationships Handbook* by Joe Biel & Dr. Faith G. Harper

- *Autism Causes Vaccines* by Joe Biel

- *The Autism Partner Handbook* by Joe Biel, Elly Blue, and Dr. Faith G. Harper

- *Good Trouble: Building a Successful Life and Business with Autism* by Joe Biel

- *The Autism Relationships Workbook: How to Thrive in Friendships, Dating, and Love* by Joe Biel & Dr. Faith G. Harper

- *The Little Book of Autism FAQs: How to Talk with Your Child about their Diagnosis and Other Conversations* by Davida Hartman

- *How to Humor with Autism* by Joe Biel

- *Asperger's Children: The Origins of Autism in Nazi Vienna* by Edith Sheffer

There are also wonderful fiction books that feature autistic characters. For example, Helen Hoang (an autistic author) writes sexy romance novels that also share the internal world of someone who is autistic and even shows wonderful ways to communicate about touch and what we like in a sexy format. Graeme Simsion's (an allistic author) *The Rosie Project* series is also beloved for it's accurate and kind portrayal of a main character who is autistic. Faith has read both these authors and can testify that they are also great writers and storytellers, so you will get a great read not just a great portrayal of an autistic person. You can find lists of all kinds of fiction with autistic characters if you are so inclined to do a Google search.

WHAT ARE YOUR SOURCES?

American Psychiatric Association Publishing. (2022). Diagnostic and statistical manual of mental disorders: Dsm-5-Tr.

Carr, M.E., Moore, D.W. & Anderson, A. Goal Setting Interventions: Implications for Participants on the Autism Spectrum. Rev J Autism Dev Disord 1, 225–241 (2014). https://doi.org/10.1007/s40489-014-0022-9

Cassidy, S., Bradley, L., Shaw, R., & Baron-Cohen, S. (2018). (2018). Suicidality and non-suicidal self-injury in adults with autism spectrum conditions. Paper presented at the International Society for Autism Research 2018 Annual Conference Program Book and Abstract Book, Rotterdam, Netherlands.

Chan, M. M., & Han, Y. M. (2020). Differential Mirror Neuron System (MNS) activation during action observation with and without social-emotional components in autism: A meta-analysis of neuroimaging studies. Molecular Autism, 11(1). https://doi.org/10.1186/s13229-020-00374-x

Chen, M. H., Pan, T. L., Lan, W. H., Hsu, J. W., Huang, K. L., Su, T. P., . . . Bai, Y. M. (2017). Risk of suicide attempts among adolescents and young adults with autism spectrum disorder: A nationwide longitudinal follow-up study. The Journal of Clinical Psychiatry, 78(9), e1174-e1179. doi:10.4088/JCP.16m11100

Centers for Disease Control and Prevention. (2022, March 31). What is autism spectrum disorder? Centers for Disease Control and Prevention. Retrieved June 9, 2022, from https://www.cdc.gov/ncbddd/autism/facts.html

Continuing to look in the Mirror: A review of neuroscientific evidence ... (n.d.). Retrieved July 20, 2022, from https://journals.sagepub.com/doi/10.1177/1362361320936945

Culpin, I., Mars, B., Pearson, R. M., Golding, J., Heron, J., Bubak, I., . . . Rai, D. (2018). Autistic traits and suicidal thoughts, plans, and self-harm in late adolescence: Population-based cohort study. Journal of the American Academy of Child and Adolescent Psychiatry, 57(5), 313-320.e6. doi:S0890-8567(18)30104-7

DeVita-Raeburn, E. (2022, August 16). The controversy over autism's most common therapy: Spectrum: Autism research news. Spectrum. Retrieved August 31, 2022, from https://www.spectrumnews.org/features/deep-dive/controversy-autisms-common-therapy/

Sinclair, J. "Don't mourn for US" - University of California, Santa Cruz. (n.d.). Retrieved August 30, 2022, from https://philosophy.ucsc.edu/SinclairDontMournForUs.pdf

Earl, R.K., Peterson, J., Wallace, A.S., Fox, E., Ma, R., Pepper, M., & Haidar, G. June 2017 Bernier Lab, Center for Human Development and Disability, University of Washington bernierlab.uw.edu

Fox, M. (2020, May 11). First US study of autism in adults estimates 2.2% have autism spectrum disorder. CNN. Retrieved July 13, 2022, from cnn.com/2020/05/11/health/autism-adults-cdc-health/index.html#:~:text=(CNN)%20The%20first%20US%20study,Control%20and%20Prevention%20said%20Monday.

Gibbs, V., Hudson, J. & Pellicano, E. The Extent and Nature of Autistic People's Violence Experiences During Adulthood: A Cross-sectional Study of Victimisation. J Autism Dev Disord (2022). https://doi.org/10.1007/s10803-022-05647-3

Gravitz, L. (2018, September). At the intersection of autism and trauma. Retrieved from https://www.spectrumnews.org/features/deep-dive/intersection-autism-tra...

Group home evicts autistic man who was shot at by police—miami herald. (n.d.). Retrieved July 20, 2022, from https://www.miamiherald.com/news/local/article236523038.html

Hall-Lande, J., Hewitt, A., Mishra, S., Piescher, K., & LaLiberte, T. (2014). Involvement of children with autism spectrum disorder (ASD) in the Child Protection System. Focus on Autism and Other Developmental Disabilities, 30(4), 237–248. https://doi.org/10.1177/1088357614539834

Head, T. (2021, August 9). 100 years of forced sterilizations in the U.S. ThoughtCo. Retrieved July 20, 2022, from https://www.thoughtco.com/forced-sterilization-in-united-states-721308

Hedley, D., Uljarević, M., Foley, K. R., Richdale, A., & Trollor, J. (2018). Risk and protective factors underlying depression and suicidal ideation in Autism Spectrum Disorder. Depression and anxiety, 35(7), 648–657. https://doi.org/10.1002/da.22759

Hirvikoski, T., Mittendorfer-Rutz, E., Boman, M., Larsson, H., Lichtenstein, P., & Bölte, S. (2016). Premature mortality in autism spectrum disorder. British Journal of Psychiatry, 208(3), 232–238. https://doi.org/10.1192/bjp.bp.114.160192

Hirvikoski, T., Boman, M., Chen, Q., D'Onofrio, B., Mittendorfer-Rutz, E., Lichtenstein, P., . . . Larsson, H. (2018). (2018). Suicidality and familial liability for suicide in autism: A population based study. Paper presented at the International Society for Autism Research 2018 Annual

Landén, M., Rasmussen, P. Gender identity disorder in a girl with autism —a case report. European Child & Adolescent Psychiatry 6, 170–173 (1997). https://doi.org/10.1007/BF00538990

Meeting Program Book and Abstract Book, Rotterdam, Netherlands. Retrieved from https://insar. confex.com/insar/2018/webprogram/Paper26787.html

Kirby, A. V., Bakian, A. V., Zhang, Y., Bilder, D. A., Keeshin, B. R., & Coon, H. (2019). A 20-year study of suicide death in a statewide autism population. Autism research : official journal of the International Society for Autism Research, 12(4), 658–666. https://doi.org/10.1002/aur.2076

Lobregt-van Buuren E, Hoekert M, Sizoo B. Autism, Adverse Events, and Trauma. In: Grabrucker AM, editor. Autism Spectrum Disorders [Internet]. Brisbane (AU): Exon Publications; 2021 Aug 20. Chapter 3. Available from: https://www.ncbi.nlm.nih.gov/books/NBK573608/ doi: 10.36255/exonpublications.autismspectrumdisorders.2021.trauma

Mayes, S. D., Gorman, A. A., Hillwig-Garcia, J., & Syed, E. (2013). Suicide ideation and attempts in children with autism. Research in Autism Spectrum Disorders, 7(1), 109–119. https://doi. org/10.1016/j.rasd.2012.07.009

McDonnell, C. G., Boan, A. D., Bradley, C. C., Seay, K. D., Charles, J. M., & Carpenter, L. A. (2019). Child maltreatment in autism spectrum disorder and intellectual disability: results from a population-based sample. Journal of child psychology and psychiatry, and allied disciplines, 60(5), 576–584. https://doi.org/10.1111/jcpp.12993

Network, M. S. I. A. (2018, July 24). The link between autism and suicide risk. The Link between Autism and Suicide Risk | Interactive Autism Network. Retrieved June 15, 2022, from https:// iancommunity.org/aic/link-between-autism-and-suicide-risk

O'Halloran, L., Coey, P., & Wilson, C. (2022). Suicidality in autistic youth: A systematic review and meta-analysis. Clinical Psychology Review, 93, 102144. https://doi.org/10.1016/j. cpr.2022.102144

Pérez Velázquez, J. L., & Galán. R. F., Information gain in the brain's resting state: A new perspective on autism. Frontiers in Neuroinformatics, 2013; 7 DOI: 10.3389/fninf.2013.00037

Publications.aap.org. (n.d.). Retrieved July 13, 2022, from https://publications.aap.org/aapnews/ news/18816/Autism-rate-rises-to-1-in-44-early-identification?searchresult=1%3Fautologinch eck

Popa-Wyatt, M. (2020). Reclamation. Grazer Philosophische Studien, 97(1), 159–176. https://doi. org/10.1163/18756735-09701009

Richa, S., Fahed, M., Khoury, E., & Mishara, B. (2014). Suicide in autism spectrum disorders. Archives of suicide research : official journal of the International Academy for Suicide Research, 18(4), 327–339. https://doi.org/10.1080/13811118.2013.824834

Smith, a. (2009). Emotional empathy in autism spectrum conditions: weak, intact or heightened? Journal of Autism Developmental Disorder, 39, 1747-1748

Rudy, L. J. (n.d.). Why do autistic children stim? Verywell Health. Retrieved September 8, 2022, from https://www.verywellhealth.com/what-is-stimming-in-autism-260034

Spencer, L., Lyketsos, C. G., Samstad, E., Dokey, A., Rostov, D., & Chisolm, M. S. (2011). A suicidal adult in crisis: An unexpected diagnosis of autism spectrum disorder. The American Journal of Psychiatry, 168(9), 890-892. doi:10.1176/appi.ajp.2011.10091261

Stagg, S. D., & Belcher, H. (2019) Living with autism without knowing: receiving a diagnosis in later life, Health Psychology and Behavioral Medicine, 7:1, 348-361, DOI: 10.1080/21642850.2019.1684920

Stavropoulos, K.K.M., Bolourian, Y., & Blacher, J. (2018). Differential Diagnosis of Autism Spectrum Disorder and Post Traumatic Stress Disorder: Two Clinical Cases. J. Clin. Med, 7, 71.

Strang, J. F., Janssen, A., Tishelman, A., Leibowitz, S. F., Kenworthy, L., McGuire, J. K., Edwards-Leeper, L., Mazefsky, C. A., Rofey, D., Bascom, J., Caplan, R., Gomez-Lobo, V., Berg, D., Zaks, Z., Wallace, G. L., Wimms, H., Pine-Twaddell, E., Shumer, D., Register-Brown, K., Sadikova, E., … Anthony, L. G. (2018). Revisiting the Link: Evidence of the Rates of Autism in Studies of Gender Diverse Individuals. Journal of the American Academy of Child and Adolescent Psychiatry, 57(11), 885–887. https://doi.org/10.1016/j.jaac.2018.04.023

The hidden danger of suicide in autism. Spectrum. (2020, August 5). Retrieved June 15, 2022, from https://www.spectrumnews.org/features/deep-dive/hidden-danger-suicide-autism/

Turban, J. L., & van Schalkwyk, G. I. (2018). "Gender Dysphoria" and Autism Spectrum Disorder: Is the Link Real?. Journal of the American Academy of Child and Adolescent Psychiatry, 57(1), 8–9.e2. https://doi.org/10.1016/j.jaac.2017.08.017

U.S. Department of Health and Human Services. (n.d.). Ask suicide-screening questions (ASQ) toolkit. National Institute of Mental Health. Retrieved June 15, 2022, from https://www.nimh.nih.gov/research/research-conducted-at-nimh/asq-toolkit-materials

van Schalkwyk, G. I., Klingensmith, K., & Volkmar, F. R. (2015). Gender identity and autism spectrum disorders. The Yale journal of biology and medicine, 88(1), 81–83.

Wang, W., Liu, J., Shi, S., Liu, T., Ma, L., Ma, X., Tian, J., Gong, Q., & Wang, M. (2018). Altered resting-state functional activity in patients with autism spectrum disorder: A quantitative meta-analysis. Frontiers in Neurology, 9. https://doi.org/10.3389/fneur.2018.00556

Warrier, V., Greenberg, D. M., Weir, E., Buckingham, C., Smith, P., Lai, M. C., Allison, C., & Baron-Cohen, S. (2020). Elevated rates of autism, other neurodevelopmental and psychiatric diagnoses, and autistic traits in transgender and gender-diverse individuals. Nature communications, 11(1), 3959. https://doi.org/10.1038/s41467-020-17794-1

Wiggins, L. D., Durkin, M. Esler, A., Lee, L., Zahorodny, W., Rice, C., Marshalyn Yeargin-Allsopp, Nicole F. Dowling, Jennifer Hall-Lande, Michael J. Morrier, Deborah Christensen, Josephine Shenouda, Jon Baio. Disparities in Documented Diagnoses of Autism Spectrum Disorder Based on Demographic, Individual, and Service Factors. Autism Research, 2019; DOI: 10.1002/aur.2255

World Health Organization. (n.d.). *Autism*. World Health Organization. Retrieved July 13, 2022, from https://www.who.int/news-room/fact-sheets/detail/autism-spectrum-disorders

World Health Organization. (2019). Icd-11: International Statistical Classification of Diseases and Related Health Problems.

WSVN, 7 N. (2022, February 16). Conviction overturned for former North Miami officer who shot at Autistic Man, injured behavioral therapist in 2016. WSVN 7News | Miami News, Weather, Sports | Fort Lauderdale. Retrieved July 20, 2022, from https://wsvn.com/news/local/conviction-overturned-for-former-north-miami-officer-who-shot-at-autistic-man-injured-behavioral-therapist-in-2016/

WHO ARE THE AUTHORS?

Joe Biel is a self-made autistic publisher and filmmaker who draws origins, inspiration, and methods from punk rock and has been featured in *Time Magazine, Publisher's Weekly, Oregonian, Spectator (Japan), G33K (Korea), and Maximum Rocknroll*. Biel is the author of dozens of books and over a hundred zines. joebiel.net

Faith Harper PhD, LPC-S, ACS, ACN is a bad-ass, funny lady with a PhD. She's a licensed professional counselor, board supervisor, certified sexologist, and applied clinical nutritionist with a private practice and consulting business in San Antonio, TX. She has been an adjunct professor and a TEDx presenter, and proudly identifies as a woman of color and uppity intersectional feminist. She is the author of dozens of books.

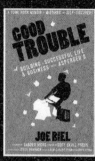

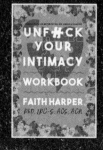